A-LEVEL PRACTICAL CHEMISTRY

Students' Guide

Brian Ratcliff

Head of Chemistry, Long Road Sixth Form College, Cambridge

CAMBRIDGE
UNIVERSITY PRESS

Published by the Press Syndicate of the University of Cambridge
The Pitt Building, Trumpington Street, Cambridge CB2 1RP
40 West 20th Street, New York, NY 10011-4211, USA
10 Stamford Road, Oakleigh, Melbourne 3166, Australia

First published 1990
Reprinted 1994

Printed in Great Britain by Athenaeum Press Ltd, Newcastle upon Tyne

British Library cataloguing in publication data
Ratcliff, Brian
  A-Level practical chemistry
  1. Chemistry, Laboratory techniques
  I. Title
  542

ISBN 0 521 37899 0 paperback

CONTENTS:

PREFACE

INTRODUCTION

1 Assessment Guidelines to Students   1
2 Techniques   7

ANALYTICAL

3 Volumetric Exercises   15
4 Qualitative Inorganic Tests   27

PHYSICAL

5 Relative Masses of Atoms and Molecules   34
6 Enthalpy Changes   39
7 Equilibria   45
8 Electrochemistry and Redox Equilibria   52
9 Rates of Reaction   59

INORGANIC

10 Periodicity   63
11 s-block Elements   69
12 Aluminium   73
13 Group IV, Carbon to Lead   75
14 Nitrogen and Sulphur   78
15 Group VII, the Halogens   81
16 Transition Elements   87

ORGANIC

17 Alkanes, Alkenes and Arenes   99
18 Alcohols and Phenol   109
19 Aldehydes and Ketones   116
20 Halogen Compounds   119
21 Carboxylic Acids and their Derivatives   124
22 Amines, Amides and Amino Acids   128

Dedicated to my wife, Barbara.

Acknowledgement is due to the following:
Homerton College Cambridge for a Teacher Associateship and the University Computer Laboratory for the use of facilities.
Cambridgeshire Education Authority for a one term secondment.
The University of Cambridge local Examinations Syndicate for permission to include the Criteria for Assessment and rewrites of two past A-level Chemistry Practical examination questions.
Dr D Johnson of Homerton College for encouragement and constructive criticism.
My colleagues, Mr P Fenwick and Mrs A Whittaker, and many of my students for constructive advice and helpful comments during the development of this work.

PREFACE.

<u>Why Practical Work?</u> There are many sound reasons for practical work in A-level Chemistry. Like other sciences, all that is known is based on the results of experimental work. A study of Chemistry without the opportunity of repeating some of this experimental work cannot convey the excitement and wonder of the subject. Much pleasure and satisfaction comes from practical work. Watching glistening crystals form from a solution or seeing the varied colours of vanadium compounds in solution can be strong aesthetic experiences. The synthesis of a compound can result in a strong sense of creative satisfaction. Most of us find that the chance to make our own observations is a powerful aid to learning.

Perhaps one of the most important reasons for practical work is the link it provides to theory. Many, otherwise abstract, theoretical concepts are given a concrete dimension and both the understanding and knowledge of theory is reinforced. Furthermore, experiments can often indicate some of the limitations of the theoretical predictions.

Many of the skills associated with the subject can only be developed through the medium of practical work. These are the skills of observation, interpretation and evaluation, planning of experiments and manipulation of apparatus. It has been argued that some of the skills taught in modern A-level Chemistry courses are irrelevant in that they are no longer used industrially or in research. Whilst this may be true, techniques such as the use of volumetric glassware encourage good manipulative skills which are transferable to other apparatus. A sound appreciation of limits of experimental error may also be developed.

Observational and interpretative skills are fundamental to the future development of any science and are indeed relevant to many areas outside the sciences. Planning exercises provide opportunities for the development of problem solving skills of a more open nature. These complement the skills needed in solving problems with more unique solutions (as in the interpretation of some practical results).

<u>Why School-based Assessment?</u> School assessment of practical work has several advantages for you as a student. In comparison to a practical examination which takes place on a single occasion, you have the benefit of assessments made on more occasions. The range of experiments set in a practical examination is, of necessity, rather narrow and much time is often needed to prepare for these during your course. School assessment makes use of experiments which are relevant to the development of your course. These factors enable a wider range of interesting experiments to be performed.

<u>How this book will help you.</u> This book endeavours to give you guidance on what will be expected of you during assessed experiments. It contains a complete course of practical work for A-level Chemistry (although it does not contain experiments on special study topics such as Biochemistry). You will only be assessed on part of the practical work you do. However, each experiment is presented as an assessed exercise so that your teacher has plenty of choice over the experiments he or she will use for your assessment mark. It also means that you have plenty of opportunity to learn what is expected and to practise.

In the first chapter you will find guidance on how you should keep your record of practical work. You will also find details of the various skills which are assessed and an indication of what is expected of you for each of these skills. In the second chapter you will find advice on the practical techniques that you will need during the course.

You will find a statement of the AIMS of the experimental work in the introduction to each topic. The introduction to each topic also contains a brief THEORY section, a SUMMARY of what you should have learned in the topic and some of the LINKS to other topics. These last two features should help to develop your understanding and knowledge of Chemistry.

v

1. ASSESSMENT GUIDELINES TO STUDENTS

1.1 Keeping records of practical work.
1.2 Observational exercises, physical and inorganic.
1.3 Observational exercises, organic.
1.4 Interpretation of results: deductive exercises.
1.5 Interpretation of results: calculations.
1.6 Designing and planning investigations.
1.7 Manipulative skills.

The criteria for the award of marks do not vary greatly between examination boards. Most schemes cover the following four skills: observation, interpretation, planning and manipulation. The four skills are given equal mark weightings by the Cambridge Board. The criteria for the award of marks presented later in this chapter are taken from the Cambridge Board syllabus.

There is often a list of the types of experiment to be included. For example, for the Cambridge Board again, the experiments must include at least one of each of the following: a titration exercise; a reaction rate experiment; a thermochemical experiment; an observational exercise; the preparation and purification of a compound.

The choice of experiments is such that each of the skills is normally assessed twice. On some occasions your teachers will use a mark scheme to mark your written work. On other occasions they will assess you during the course of a practical lesson. They may watch how you carry out specific tasks or they may carry out some oral assessment.

If you are absent for an assessment, there will be other occasions on which you may be assessed. Your teachers do not have to assess everybody in your class on the same eight experiments. They may well do quite a few more than eight to cover absences or to enable them to ignore a single, uncharactistically poor mark by an individual student.

1.1 KEEPING RECORDS OF PRACTICAL WORK.

Scientific progress relies on the methodical reporting of experimental work. The laboratory notes of famous scientists can have much value. Quite apart from their value to collectors or their historical interest, they provide important reference material for other scientists. Not only do they enable results to be confirmed but they pave the way for future discoveries.

Your own record of practical work may not seem to have such great importance. Nevertheless, you should take considerable care recording both what you do and how you interpret your results. A clear record of practical results helps considerably when it comes to their interpretion. You will also find that your laboratory notes become an important source of reference as the A-level course progresses. You will find your practical record useful when planning experiments, when interpreting results or for revision. If you have aspirations to become a great scientist you must learn to record your work, otherwise nobody will learn about your discoveries for you to become famous!

At a very mundane level, the A-level examining board may need to see your practical record for moderation purposes. HENCE YOU MUST KEEP ALL YOUR PRACTICAL NOTES. Moderation is carried out to ensure that standards of marking in different schools are comparable. Differences in marking standards between schools may be removed by adjusting the marks for the schools concerned.

1

<u>What you need to do</u>: You will probably find it easiest to use an A4 ring binder. You can then use this to keep together completed copies of the tables provided, your interpretations of results, methods proposed for planning exercises, etc. Normally you are not expected to write out the method for a particular experiment if this is given in the text. However, it would be good sense to make a summary note of the method for each experiment for your own reference and revision.

It is expected that you will write down your results neatly and clearly, in ink, as they are obtained. It is bad practice, and a waste of your time, to rewrite your results. Before you start a practical read through the procedure and plan your presentation of results as necessary. Do not use abbreviations, except those approved for units.

Remember to put your name and the date on all your work.

1.2 OBSERVATIONAL EXERCISES, PHYSICAL AND INORGANIC.

All experimental work requires careful recording of results. Remember to write your results down as they are obtained in their final form. This is particularly important for numerical quantities. Numerical measurements made in physical chemistry experiments are observations that need to be made with care. They should be checked after writing them down. Do not write them down in rough before transferring them to your full write up, they may be omitted or confused. Write them down as you make a reading. Remember to take your practical record with you to the balance when weighing, do not try to remember figures in your head as you walk back to your bench!

Observational exercises involving test tube reactions need to be relevant, concise yet complete. Be on the look out for the unexpected. An impersonal style is preferred by some teachers (see examples, below). Remember: the only acceptable abbreviations are for units.

Difficulties commonly encountered by students:

(1) Recognising relevant and irrelevant observations.

   (a) For example it is possible to add solutions to a test tube in such a manner that layers of reagent form. Reaction will only occur at the boundaries, probably giving a banded appearance. Remember to mix your reagents thoroughly before describing your observations.

   (b) Another type of observation which may not be directly relevant may be caused by the reaction of two chemicals added to your original sample; e.g. addition of zinc and dilute hydrochloric acid to your sample will produce hydrogen. This occurs whether you have your sample present or not.

(2) Failure to carry out the instructions. When you think you have completed the test, check the instructions again. Have you missed anything?

(3) Gases - describe colour, odour, effect on damp litmus and then carry out a confirmatory test.

(4) Samples of solid reagent too large. Solids contain much greater amounts of substance than solutions. Use them sparingly. You will see a small amount dissolve more easily and quickly than a larger amount. A large amount may be in excess and thus hide what you should see.

(5) There are circumstances where you may not be sure if a change has occurred. In these instances use a control consisting of distilled water for comparison.

(6) If you are adding acid to a solution already made alkaline, check that you have added sufficient acid to neutralise the alkali. Similarly check you have added sufficient alkali if the solution was aleady acidic.

(7) Finally do make sure that you have carried out the instructions correctly and completely.

2

Examples of observational records.

Gas evolution: A colourless gas with a pungent odour was evolved.
The gas turned pink litmus paper blue.
IS BETTER THAN:
Mixture fizzes off a strong smelling gas. Test with
litmus shows gas is alkaline.

The second observation has several things wrong.
The litmus test is not clear, it is not an observation but a deduction.
The standard of English is also poor.

Colour changes: The blue solution was decolorised.
IS BETTER THAN:
The blue solution went clear.

What does the word clear mean? Surely the solution was
clear when it was blue? The opposite of clear is cloudy.

Precipitates: An off-white precipitate formed.
IS BETTER THAN:
The solution became dirty white.

It is not clear if a precipitate has formed. Is it "dirty"?

Criteria for Assessment: Observing, Measuring and Recording.

Marks are awarded as follows:

1

2   Given guidance, makes and records some relevant observations or readings.

3

4   Makes and records relevant observations or measurements.

5

6   Makes and records a full range of relevant observations or measurements to an
           appropriate degree of accuracy.

1.3 OBSERVATIONAL EXERCISES, ORGANIC.

Much of what appears in 1.2 above applies to organic observational exercises.

However organic test tube reactions do bring their own special difficuties.

(1) Often organic chemicals are volatile liquids. As with solids, the amount of compound
     present is much greater than when solutions are used. Hence they should be used sparingly.

(2) As liquids they may be immiscible or partially immiscible in water. This will give rise to
     more than one liquid layer on mixing with aqueous reagents. Emulsions may form, these
     may look like precipitates. Surface tension may cause droplets to float on water with the
     denser organic liquid at the bottom of the tube.

(3) Most organic compounds have distinctive odours. These can be very confusing to the
     inexperienced. Try to group odours together, e.g. fruity, sweet, acid, pleasant, unpleasant,
     antiseptic etc. Whilst many of these descriptions are subjective, you will gradually learn the
     type of odour associated with a particular type of compound.

Criteria for Assessment: these are given in section 1.2 above.

1.4 INTERPRETATION OF RESULTS: DEDUCTIVE EXERCISES.

The observations that you make during the course of your experiments will provide you with many clues. You may have sufficient clues to make inferences about the substances present or the reactions occurring. You may find that you need further clues in order to confirm these inferences. Imagine that you are a detective trying to solve a crime - do the clues that you have point to one possibility or several? Is there anything that you have not considered? How good is the evidence for your deductions? Try to consider the significance of what is being observed as you go along. Do not blindly follow instructions, but ask yourself why you are adding particular reagents. What type of reagents are you mixing? What sort of reaction could occur?

In many of the observational exercises in this book, these and similar questions are provided to guide your thinking. Your progress will be better if you make sure that you learn reactions as you meet them. You will find that the interpretation of results in similar situations is much easier as your knowledge increases. Many research chemists believe that intuition can be helpful in interpretation. Certainly, the transfer of understanding from one situation to another may help considerably. This can only occur if you have learnt earlier material thoroughly.

Finally do beware of red herrings. These are deductions made from observations which would be seen even in the absence of the compound in which you are interested. See, for example, section 1.2 part (1)(b) on p2.

Criteria for Assessment: Interpreting Experimental Observations and Data.

Marks are awarded as follows:

1

2   Draws a simple conclusion from the results of an experiment.

3

4   Draws a conclusion which is consistent with a series of results.

5

6   Expresses conclusions as generalisations or patterns where appropriate.
           Able to appreciate:
           (i) the limitations of an experiment,
           (ii) when it is necesary to obtain further results.

1.5 INTERPRETATION OF RESULTS: CALCULATIONS.

Marks are lost for a variety of reasons:

(1)   Inability to complete the calculation. Take heart! Many of the calculations you will be expected to do are structured in such a way that you may well obtain 60% of the marks available without completing them! If you are absolutely stuck, seek help from your teachers - you may lose a mark but they may see your difficulty and be able to point you in the right direction for you to gain several more marks!

(2)   You have the right answer but important steps are missing on the way there. Take note of the methods you are shown. Does each step in your calculation logically lead on to the next? Does your answer look sensible numerically?

(3)   Omission of units, incorrect units. Check these carefully, they frequently carry marks.

Criteria for Assessment: see section 1.4 above.

1.6 DESIGNING AND PLANNING INVESTIGATIONS.

You will normally be expected to write out a method which could be followed by another A-level student. Note carefully the several ways in which this is done in the procedures given in this text. There will probably be a suitable model for you. Don't jump at your first idea, think on! You may have a better idea for a method. You may normally use your notes and your teacher as a resource. You are not being tested on your knowledge of facts at this stage. You will probably be asked to try out your method. When you do so, you may find ways in which to improve your suggested plan. Make sure that you notify your teacher of any modifications that you put into practice. Record them in your write-up.

Marks are lost for impractical methods, inappropriate techniques and failure to specify quantities. If there are weighings or volumes, clearly these must be specified. You may have to do some calculations to decide what is appropriate. For example: if you are finding the enthalpy change when a metal dissolves in an acid, you would need to calculate what mass of metal would react completely with a chosen volume of acid. To ensure complete reaction the acid would be in excess. Your weighing of the metal would be in vain if it did not all dissolve!

Normally, methods expected will be drawn from those in your A-level experience. Think carefully about techniques, e.g. if you are adding an excess of an acid during a redox titration, what is the most appropriate glassware to use to measure the volume? Is it a burette, pipette or measuring cylinder?

Criteria for Assessment: Designing and Planning Investigations.

Marks are awarded as follows:

1

2   Is able to suggest a simple plan to carry out an investigation.
Attempts "trial and error" modifications in the light of the experience.

3

4   (a) Suggests a sound plan requiring little modification.

       (b) Comments critically on the original plan, and implements appropriate changes in the light of experience. (Note that only one of (a) or (b) needs to be satisfied.)

5

6   Plans efficiently and times the various parts realistically; capable of modifying the plan in the light of experience.

1.7 MANIPULATIVE SKILLS.

Your teachers will assess you during the course of a practical lesson. They will look at your organisation and your proficiency in handling apparatus. They may have a tick list covering key points. If they use this you will gain marks where they see you performing correctly.

Some examples follow of what they might be looking for when marking this way.

Apparatus in general: Equipment suitably positioned on the bench so that the experiment may be conducted safely and comfortably. Bunsen burners placed back from the edge of the bench (suggest approximately 30 cm). Rubber tubing arranged clear of bunsen burners and free of kinks. Necessary apparatus collected together quickly at the start of an experiment in order to make the best use of the time available.

Electrical apparatus (see also 2.10): Circuits made neatly so that they are clear and there is less chance of confusion over connections. All electrical equipment arranged well clear of chemicals, especially of solutions. Meters placed for easy reading.

Test tube experiments: Suitable quantities of solid, liquid or solution used. Teat pipettes used correctly (see 2.2.1). Substances adequately mixed by shaking using wrist action or by stirring with a glass rod (not thumb over end of tube!). Tube contents shaken when heated, care taken to point mouth of tube away from self and neighbours (see 2.2.3).

Weighings: Might include: Turning balance off when changing weights or placing sample on pan (depending on type of balance). Use of appropriate container to weigh sample. Care when adding sample to container to avoid spillage. Clearing up any spillage and speed of weighing.

Titrations (see also 2.3): Burette - jet full of solution; eye level with meniscus when taking readings; good tap control, able to add single drops of solution; filter funnel used for filling not left in burette. Pipette - no air bubbles present; allowed to drain naturally; solution surface or side of container touched for correct drainage of last drop. Flask - rinsed thoroughly with distilled water between titrations; swirled during additions from burette; correct end-point taken.

They may also use the internal consistency of your own titration results, together with their agreement with the result determined by themselves or the laboratory technician.

Other ways in which they may assess your manipulative skills include looking at the accuracy and consistency of your results. For example they might expect you to obtain titration values within $\pm$ 0.1 cm^3. If you have prepared an organic solid, they might assess its purity by means of its melting point.

Criteria for Assessment: Using and Organising Techniques, Apparatus and Materials.

Marks are awarded as follows:

1

2   With guidance, can perform a simple practical operation using familiar apparatus and materials adequately.

3

4   Adequate ability, generally able to apply an appropriate degree of precision to particular manipulations.

5

6   Full range of skills well displayed. Experiment carried out efficiently and to a suitable degree of accuracy without assistance.

2. TECHNIQUES

2.1 Safety.
2.2 Test tube techniques.
2.3 Use of volumetric glassware.
2.4 Glassware with interchangeable ground glass joints.
2.5 Recrystallisation.
2.6 Buchner filtration.
2.7 Determination of a melting point.
2.8 Use of a separating funnel.
2.9 Drying liquids.
2.10 Using electrical equipment.
2.11 Quantifiable errors.

2.1 SAFETY.

Whenever you work in a Chemistry laboratory, you must always keep within clearly defined guidelines. Your teacher will explain just what is expected in your own school.

YOU SHOULD WEAR SAFETY GOGGLES FOR ALL PRACTICAL WORK INVOLVING CHEMICALS.

There may be circumstances where this is not strictly necessary, but such occasions are rare. The only sound advice is to wear your goggles whenever you are in the laboratory and chemicals are being used.

You are also strongly advised to wear a laboratory coat to protect your clothing from chemical splashes.

HAZARD WARNINGS: TREAT ALL CHEMICALS WITH RESPECT. In the past people have used chemicals such as benzene with little or no safety precautions. It is only in relatively recent years that the dangers of benzene have been appreciated. You may be using a chemical whose dangers have not yet been realised.

YOU WILL FIND THAT WHERE PARTICULAR HAZARDS ARE INVOLVED IN EXPERIMENTS IN THIS BOOK, THESE ARE DETAILED IN ITALICS, LIKE THESE, AT THE START OF THE EXPERIMENT.

BE SURE TO FOLLOW SAFETY INSTRUCTIONS CAREFULLY.

Use of Fume Cupboard: Many hazardous gases or volatile liquids must only be handled in an efficient fume cupboard. It is a good rule to use a fume cupboard if there is any doubt about the safety of a chemical. Where the use of a fume cupboard is essential this is indicated. *The front of the cupboard should only be opened as far as the indicated height for safe working. You must NOT work with your head inside the cupboard!*

2.2 TEST-TUBE TECHNIQUES.

2.2.1 ADDING REAGENTS.

When using teat pipettes, be careful to avoid cross-contamination of reagents. You should hold the pipette so that the jet is just above the mouth of the test tube. If the pipette jet touches the inside walls of the test tube, it may carry reagent back to the stock bottle. This may cause spurious results in a later test.

Also, hold the bulb of the teat between thumb and forefinger. Place your second and third fingers under the pipette tube. This enables you to add drops of reagent as steadily as possible.

It is good practice to keep a teat pipette in a beaker of distilled water ready for use. After use

7

rinse the pipette and replace in the beaker. You then know it is clean and ready for future use.

2.2.2 MIXING.
Do not place your thumb over the end and shake! Develop a swirling action, controlled mainly by wrist movement. Ask your teacher to show you.

Alternatively stir gently with a glass rod. Keep a glass rod with your teat pipette in a beaker of distilled water (see 2.2.1).

2.2.3 HEATING.
Do not point your test tube at anybody in case the contents are ejected. Keep the tube moving to avoid this possibility. Look out for thick precipitates, these may cause excessive bumping and ejection of the contents of the tube.

2.2.4 TESTING GASES.
Always note colour, odour, action on damp litmus paper and effect on a lighted splint.

Take care when smelling a gas, many are poisonous and they can cause irritation. The correct technique is to gently waft the gas towards your nose from the top of the test tube. Avoid inhaling gases.

To bubble a gas through a liquid use a clean teat pipette. Squeeze the air out of the teat and gently draw up the gas from just above the surface of the reaction mixture in the test tube. Now squeeze the teat, expelling the gas through the chosen test solution. Flush the pipette once or twice with this solution. Keep a clean teat pipette ready for use with the glass rod in the beaker of water.

The best method for burning hydrogen is to collect some in a boiling tube inverted over the test tube where the gas is being produced. When you have collected sufficient gas, move the boiling tube over to a bunsen flame. Keep the mouth of the tube covered with your hand whilst you do this. Remove your hand and tip the tube so that the hydrogen escapes into the flame. This method can produce a good "pop". A glowing splint placed in the test tube where oxygen is being produced may ignite with an audible pop.

2.2.5 USING ORGANIC REAGENTS.
Odours frequently cause difficulty. Hold the test tube near your nose and gently waft the odour towards you with your hand. (See also 1.3.) Try to relate odours to those you have come across in everyday life.

HAZARD WARNING: ORGANIC WASTE IS OFTEN HIGHLY FLAMMABLE! Disposal of organic waste. There are two categories: water soluble and water insoluble. The insoluble volatile liquid waste should be collected together in a beaker in the fume cupboard. The easiest way of disposing of this is to allow it to evaporate in a well ventilated space. Pour water soluble waste down the fume cupboard sink, followed by plenty of water.

2.3 USE OF VOLUMETRIC GLASSWARE.

2.3.1 PIPETTE.
HAZARD WARNING: YOU MUST USE A SAFETY FILLER - NEVER YOUR MOUTH.

The pipette should first be rinsed with a small quantity of the solution to be measured. Discard the rinse solution. Using a safety filler, draw the solution to above the mark. Allow to run out until the meniscus is on the graduated mark. Check that no air bubbles are present, especially at the jet. If you use your finger after filling for levelling, try rotating the pipette whilst pressing your finger on the end. You will find this gives much better control. Never use your thumb. Wipe any drops of solution from the outside wall of the pipette. Allow the solution to drain naturally and touch the surface of the drained solution with the jet. This allows the correct retention of the last drop of solution by the pipette.

2.3.2 BURETTE.

Rinse this with the solution you are going to put in it, make sure you rinse through the tap and jet. Discard the rinse solution. Fill the burette to above the 0.0 cm^3 mark. Run out solution to fill the tap and jet, check no air is trapped in the jet. There is no need to to adjust the volume of solution to exactly 0.00 cm^3. This wastes time and is bad practice. Remember to remove the filter funnel if you have used one.

2.3.3 THE TITRATION FLASK.

You will normally use a 250 cm^3 conical flask. It should be thoroughly rinsed with distilled water before use and between titrations. During a titration, rinse down splashes on the sides of the flask, with a little distilled water from a wash bottle.

2.3.4 THE VOLUMETRIC FLASK.

This should be rinsed with distilled water before use. If you are dissolving an accurately weighed solid sample you must ensure that all the sample is transferred to the flask. The correct way to do this is to transfer the solid from the weighing tube to a clean beaker. Wash the tube at least three times with distilled water, adding the washings to the beaker. Now add enough water to dissolve the solid. Warm if necessary. Cool and transfer the solution to the volumetric flask. Wash the beaker at least three times with distilled water, transferring the washings to the volumetric flask. Now make up to the mark with distilled water. Add the water in drops when close to the mark.

2.3.5 THE MENISCUS.

Always remember to sight along the meniscus at eye level.

2.3.6 INDICATORS.

Follow instructions for use carefully, sometimes a drop is needed, sometimes up to a cubic centimetre.

2.3.7 CLEANING GLASSWARE AFTER USE.

All glassware should be thoroughly rinsed with tap water followed by three rinses with distilled water. When you use potassium manganate(VII), note how many rinses are needed to remove all traces of colour. Leave burettes upside down in stands with the taps open. Place pipette in rack to drain.

2.4 GLASSWARE WITH INTERCHANGEABLE GROUND GLASS JOINTS.

You will seldom find glassware connected by corks or rubber bungs in a modern chemical laboratory. Glassware with interchangeable ground glass joints has become almost universally used, even in school laboratories for A-level work. It is not difficult to see the reasons for this.

The advantages of such glassware include:
- greater ease of handling,
- no cork or rubber bungs to corrode,
- no bungs to introduce impurities,
- a good fit obtainable at the joints,
- greater speed of assembly and dismantling,
- wider passages in condensers etc. reduce risk of blockage.

Disadvantages include:
- joints must be clean and free from grit (light greasing needed),
- joints may stick together if alkali used (should be dismantled after use),
- much greater cost!

ASSEMBLY:

(1) Very lightly grease the joints. Apply a smear of silicone grease to the cones. Too much grease is difficult to remove and leaves the glass looking dirty.

(2) Choose a suitable starting point from which to build up your apparatus. This will usually be the reaction flask.

(3) Using a clamp with rubber lined jaws, secure the flask gently round the socket.

(4) Insert the next item (e.g. reflux condenser, still head) in the flask. Attach rubber tubing to condensers first. To do this wet the end of the tube, hold the condenser near to a nipple and push the rubber tube on with a twisting motion. Ask your teacher to show you if you are not sure.

(5) A distillation condenser is best secured by a clamp to the same retort stand as that holding the flask. This will require the use of a variable boss which can be set at an appropriate angle. Such an arrangement will avoid the condenser separating slightly from the rest of the apparatus. You will also find it easier to move your apparatus around if only one retort stand is used.

(6) Cleaning. After use, reaction flasks may require the use of a test tube brush. Be sure to rinse the apparatus thoroughly with distilled water. If you have been using organic chemicals, you may need to use a solvent such as propanone or industrial methylated spirits. Check the glassware for organic odours and rinse with a solvent if necessary. Do not waste solvent, a little may be used for several items.

2.5 RECRYSTALLISATION.

This technique is frequently used to purify a solid.

A solid is dissolved in a suitable hot solvent and the solution cooled. Pure solid crystallises leaving the impurities in solution if they are more soluble or if there is less of them.

It is important to choose a solvent in which the solid to be purified is reasonably soluble when hot but considerably less soluble when cold. There is considerable art to the technique. It requires a fine judgement of the amount of solvent to use. The aim is to use just enough to dissolve the solid when the mixture is hot. This will enable the maximum amount to crystallise on cooling. Cooling in ice may also be needed.

(1) Dissolve the impure solid compound in the minimum of the hot solvent. Do this by placing the solid in a conical flask, and adding hot solvent, a little at a time. It may be necessary to warm the flask.

(2) Some solids with low melting points may form an oil. Watch out for this, you will need to add more solvent until the oil has been dissolved.

(3) Check the solution is free of dust or filter paper. If it is not it will need filtering, possibly through a heated funnel.

(4) Leave the solution to cool undisturbed, watch out for the crystals to form. Occasionally supercooling occurs and no crystals form, the solution becoming supersaturated. If this occurs shaking the flask may be all that is required to start rapid crystallisation. Alternatively scratching the side with a glass rod or adding a small, seed crystal may initiate crystallisation.

(5) Fractional crystallisation is needed where compounds have similar solubilities or are present in similar amounts. This may involve repetition of the crystallisation process. Careful choice of the volume of solvent used may enable separation with just one recrystallisation.

2.6 BUCHNER FILTRATION.

If the pressure is reduced on the flask side of a filter funnel, air pressure causes more rapid flow of filtrate through the paper. One type of apparatus for this is shown in figure 1.

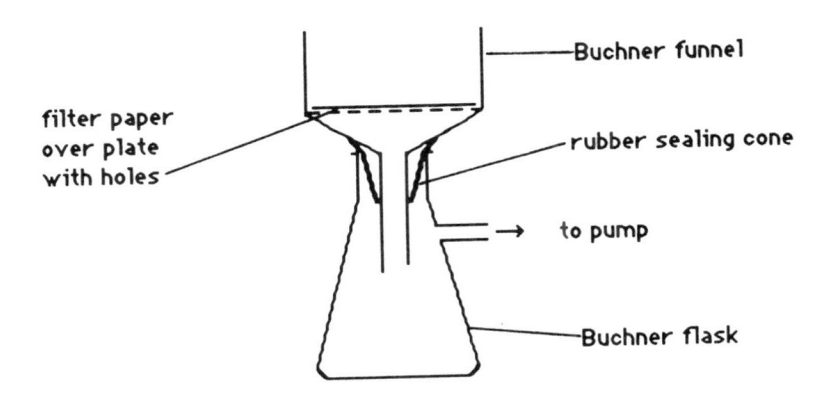

Figure 1: A Buchner Filter.

To set up the funnel for filtration, a filter paper with a similar diameter to the flat bottom of the funnel is needed. If necessary, a larger filter paper must be cut to size. This is placed so that the holes in the funnel are covered. The paper is then moistened with a few drops of the solvent used in the solution to be filtered.

The funnel is placed in the rubber cone in the flask and connected to a water (or other suitable) pump. It may be necessary to press down on the funnel to help it seal with the rubber. It also helps to clamp the flask.

The mixture to be filtered is then directed on to the centre of the filter paper by pouring it down a glass rod, whilst applying suction with the pump. Before doing this swirl the mixture so that crystals are carried into the funnel. It may be necessary to scrape out the remaining crystals into the funnel using a glass rod. Alternatively, some of the filtrate may be returned to the flask containing the crystals to help wash them all out.

Once the filtrate has passed into the Buchner flask, continue drawing air through the funnel to dry the crystals for a few minutes. Do not wash the crystals unless you are told to do so in the experiment.

The filter paper and crystals may now be removed and drying completed in air (or in an oven or desiccator). When removing crystals from the filter paper, avoid scratching at the paper as this will remove cellulose fibres as well as the crystals.

2.7 DETERMINATION OF A MELTING POINT.

(1) The sample for the melting point determination should be dry. If it is crystalline it may first need grinding (or crushing) to a powder.

(2) A thin walled glass melting point tube is sealed at one end. Do this by heating the end in a blue bunsen flame, rotate the tube whilst heating.

(3) Cool the tube and introduce some of the sample. Gently tap the tube to settle the sample to the lower, sealed end of the tube. You need sufficient sample to see clearly.

(4) Attach the melting point tube to a thermometer of suitable range using a small rubber ring cut from rubber tubing. The sample and sealed end should be close to the thermometer bulb.

(5) The thermometer is inserted through a cork with a groove cut at the side (CARE!).

(6) The thermometer assembly is now placed in a Thiele tube (see figure 2). This should contain water for melting points below 100 °C or a paraffin oil for melting points above 100 °C. If Thiele tubes are not available a hard glass boiling tube may be used, this however will also require a stirrer. The thermometer bulb and sample should be submerged and level with the upper arm of the Thiele tube.

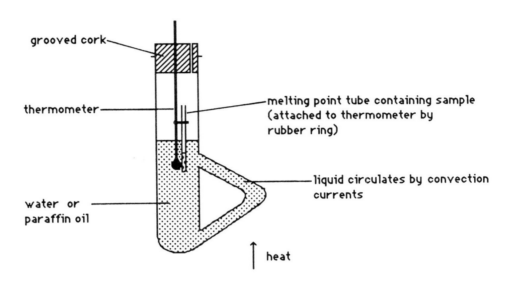

grooved cork

thermometer

melting point tube containing sample (attached to thermometer by rubber ring)

liquid circulates by convection currents

water or paraffin oil

heat

Figure 2: Melting Point Apparatus.

(7) Heat the Thiele tube gently with a small bunsen flame at the elbow of the side arm. The oil or water will circulate round the tube by convection.

(8) Watch the sample closely and note the temperature melting starts and ends.

(9) Repeat the melting point determination with a fresh sample.

(10) If the substance is recrystallised again, it may be found to have a slightly higher, sharper melting point. This is because impurities have the effect of lowering the melting point and making it less sharp.

2.8 USE OF A SEPARATING FUNNEL.

A diagram of a separating funnel is given in figure 3. Its main use is for the separation of two immiscible liquids. Such a separation may follow the extraction of an organic solute from water using a solvent such as ethoxyethane (a process known as Solvent Extraction). A separating funnel may also be used during the purification of a liquid product (e.g. for neutralising acid present etc.). The separation is carried out as follows.

(1) Check that the ground glass joints are lightly greased and the tap is securely closed.

(2) The mixture of solvents is placed in the separating funnel.

(3) Solvent Extraction or Purification. The funnel is stoppered, the stopper held firmly in place with a forefinger and the funnel inverted. Shaking the mixture will ensure adequate equilibration of the solute between the two solvents. The equilibrium constant for this

12

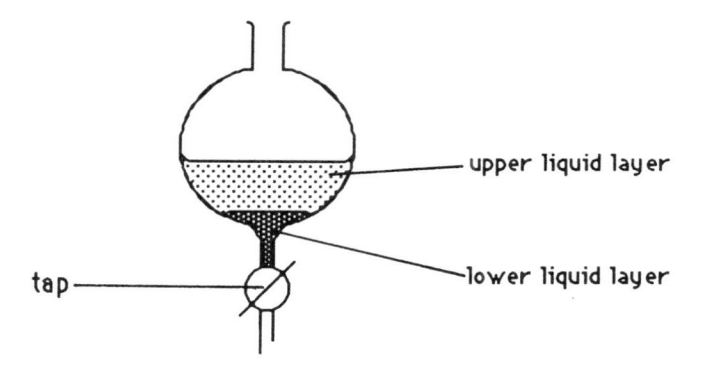

Figure 3: A Separating Funnel.

process is known as the partition (or distribution) coefficient.

(4) During stage (3), pressure may build up in the funnel due to the volatility of the organic solvent. This is released through the tap whilst the funnel is inverted. In this way any liquid expelled can be allowed to drain back into the funnel.

(5) The funnel is now placed in a stand and the contents allowed to settle. This may take a few minutes.

(6) Decide which layer is to be kept. Refer to density tables in a data book if necessary. Remove the stopper and drain the lower layer into a clean flask. Close the tap so that the meniscus between the two layers is caught in the tap.

(7) If the upper layer is required this is poured out of the top of the funnel. This avoids contamination with the last trace of lower liquid layer in the tap.

2.9 DRYING LIQUIDS.

After extraction in a separating funnel a solution in an organic solvent may require drying before final separation by distillation. The solution is placed in a suitable conical flask and a small quantity of a drying agent added. The flask is stoppered, the mixture swirled and allowed to stand. Any initial cloudiness due to water should disappear leaving a clear solution and solid drying agent. If drops of water are present more drying agent may be needed. However, careful use of the separating funnel should avoid this.

Various drying agents are employed. These include anhydrous calcium chloride and anhydrous magnesium sulphate. After drying, the clear solution is best filtered through a small plug of glass wool to remove the drying agent.

2.10 USING ELECTRICAL EQUIPMENT.

Meters, such as pH/mV meters, are expensive. Most electrical equipment can be seriously, perhaps irreparably, damaged if it comes into contact with chemicals. Take care when you are setting up your apparatus to place all sensitive equipment well away from chemicals, particularly solutions.

You should be able to set up a circuit following a simple circuit diagram. Where necessary you must observe the correct polarity of leads and electrodes. You should be familiar with the use of an ammeter (0–1 A), voltmeter and rheostat as well as the more specialised apparatus you will meet in your A-level Chemistry course.

2.11 QUANTIFIABLE ERRORS.

Several types of error are recognisable:

(1) Operator errors, due to carelessness or misuse of apparatus. Careful work is needed at all times. Errors due to misreading apparatus can be avoided if figures are written down at the apparatus and checked. Such errors cannot be quantified.

(2) Instrument calibration. Different readings may be obtained using different samples of the same equipment. This is particularly true of thermometers. If absolute values of temperature are required rather than differences it may be necessary to check the readings of thermometers against each other. Cheap thermometers may vary by 0.5 to 1 °C. However the error when temperature differences are measured may be reasonably ignored.

(3) Precision errors. This is the only type which shows a reasonable degree of experimental reproducibility. Such errors may therefore be quantified. Individual pieces of equipment will be built to specified standards. The higher the degree of precision, the greater the cost. Some examples: Balance - different types with ranges of precision from 0.1 g to 0.0001 g may be available in your school laboratories. Measuring cylinder - a 100 cm^3 cylinder will usually enable a volume to be measured to 1 cm^3. Pipette, burette - will measure volume to 0.1 cm^3 if it is of type B. (Type A pipettes and burettes are much more expensive but will measure volumes to 0.05 cm^3.) Thermometer - most measure to 1 °C. For heats of reaction you will use a thermometer with a precision of 0.1 or 0.2 °C.

Uncertainties in readings should be recorded by using ± or significant figures. e.g. 36.3 ± 0.1 °C or 25.00 cm^3.

Treatment of Errors in Calculations.

(1) **Adding or subtracting measured quantities.** The maximum absolute uncertainty is the sum of the individual uncertainties:

e.g. if the numerical values of two temperatures are 36.3 ± 0.1 and 56.3 ± 0.1, the difference is 20.0 ± 0.2. The first temperature may be as low as 36.2, the second as high as 56.4 giving a maximum difference of 20.2.

(2) **Multiplying or dividing measured quantities.** The maximum fractional or percentage uncertainty is the sum of the percentage uncertainties for each of the individual quantities:

e.g. the heat capacity of a calorimeter is 50 ± 1 J K^{-1} and in an experiment a temperature rise of 4.0 ± 0.2 K is obtained.

The error in the heat capacity is 1 J K^{-1}, i.e. 1/50 x 100 % = 2%.

The error in the temperature reading is 0.2/4.0 x 100 % = 5%

The maximum percentage uncertainty in the amount of heat energy released is thus:

$$2 + 5 = 7\%$$

i.e. Heat energy released = 50 x 4.0 J = 200 ± 14 J, as 7% of 200 is 14.

(Alternatively you may do the same estimate using the fractional errors rather than percentage errors. As with percentage errors, total fractional error is the sum of the individual fractional errors.)

14

3. VOLUMETRIC EXERCISES

3.1 Introduction to volumetric exercises.
3.2 Calculations for volumetric exercises.
3.3 Acid/base titrations.
    3.3.1 The concentration of ethanoic acid in vinegar.
    3.3.2 Determination of the number of moles of water of crystallisation in a borate.
    3.3.3 The efflorescence of washing soda crystals.
    3.3.4 A titration with two indicators.
3.4 Redox titrations.
    3.4.1 The equation for the reaction of iodate(V) with iodide.
    3.4.2 Determination of sodium chlorate(I) in bleach.
    3.4.3 The standardisation of potassium manganate(VII).
    3.4.4 The aerial oxidation of aqueous iron(II) sulphate.

3.1 INTRODUCTION TO VOLUMETRIC EXERCISES.

AIMS: These exercises introduce you to a traditional analytical technique. They are intended to develop good manipulative skills. They also provide you with practice at calculations involving concentrations. Quantitative aspects of Chemistry from other parts of the course are illustrated.

THEORY: A molar solution contains one mole of compound dissolved in one cubic decimetre (units $mol\ dm^{-3}$). (N.B. one decimetre is 10 cm, so one cubic decimetre is $10 \times 10 \times 10\ cm^3$ or $1000\ cm^3$.) As we weigh in grams, we can also measure concentration in number of grams of compound in one cubic decimetre (units $g\ dm^{-3}$).

Standard solutions are solutions whose exact concentrations are known. They may be made by dissolving an accurately weighed mass of compound in water and carefully making up to a known volume using a graduated flask. (See subsection 2.3.4). However, many substances cannot easily be accurately weighed. For example concentrated acids contain some water and some solid substances absorb water whilst being weighed. Solutions of such substances are standardised by titration against a compound which can be accurately weighed and made up into a solution.

SUMMARY: At the end of this topic you should be able to:

(1)   manipulate volumetric glassware to a high standard,

(2)   perform calculations based on the results of titration exercises,

(3)   quantify errors due to the limitations of the apparatus that you are using,

(4)   plan your own titration experiments.

LINKS: Use is made of titrations in other topics, for example Equilibria (Topic 7) and Rates of Reaction (Topic 9). In this topic material from other topics is illustrated quantitatively. Examples of exercises relevant to many different topics will be found.

3.2 CALCULATIONS FOR VOLUMETRIC EXERCISES.

Calculations for volumetric exercises make use of a few basic steps.

The steps found in the calculations may involve the following:

(1)   Choice of Titre: The volume (titre) that you use from your titration figures must be taken from your accurate values. NEVER use your rough value. You should aim at obtaining at least three accurate titres which differ by no more than $\pm\ 0.1\ cm^3$.

   If you have obtained two accurate titres which are the same, use this consistent titre for your calculation (e.g. if you obtain 23.20, 23.25, 23.25 cm^3 then use 23.25 cm^3).

If you obtain three values which differ by ± 0.1 cm³ then take the average of these three (e.g. for 25.10, 25.00, 25.20 cm³ use 25.10 cm³).

If you have a titre which differs from your other results by ± 0.2 cm³ or more, then ignore this titre. In this case you should ensure you have three other accurate titres to use. Carry out another titration if necessary. (e.g. 26.35, 26.10, 26.40, 26.45 cm³ use 26.40 and ignore 26.10 as this latter titre is inconsistent with the other three titres.)

(2) Scaling quantities up or down.

(a) What amount of hydroxide ion is present in 24.0 cm³ of a 0.010 mol dm⁻³ solution?

$$24 \text{ cm}^3 = \frac{24}{1000} \text{ dm}^3$$

(converts volume to correct units for concentration.)

$$\text{Amount of OH}^- \text{ ion} = \frac{24}{1000} \times 0.010 = 2.4 \times 10^{-4} \text{ mol}$$

(check original volume, should the answer be greater or smaller than the numerical value of concentration?)

(b) What is the concentration of a solution containing 2×10^{-4} mol of manganate(VII) ion in 10 cm³?

$$\text{Concentration of MnO}_4^- \text{ ions} = \frac{1000}{10} \times 2 \times 10^{-4} \text{ mol dm}^{-3}$$

(We are given the moles in 10 cm³ and wish to know the moles in 1 dm³, i.e. 1000 cm³. Again check - should the answer be greater or smaller than the numerical value of concentration?)

This is essentially the reverse of the method for (a). Remember the abbreviation for moles is mol, the unit for amount of substance. You will sometimes see the symbol M; this stands for molarity. Avoid using this symbol in all calculation work. Its use in calculations can be a source of error and confusion. It is useful when labelling bottles and in other places where brevity is needed.

(3) Conversion of g dm⁻³ to mol dm⁻³ and vice versa.

(a) What is the concentration of a solution containing 4.00 g of NaOH in one cubic decimetre?

M_r of NaOH is 23 + 16 + 1 = 40

Hence concentration of NaOH is $\frac{4.00}{40} = 0.10$ mol dm⁻³

(b) What is the concentration in g dm⁻³ of 0.50 mol dm⁻³ ethanoic acid?

M_r of ethanoic acid, CH_3CO_2H, is 12 + 3 + 12 + 32 + 1 = 60

Hence concentration of ethanoic acid = 0.50 × 60 = 30.0 g dm⁻³

In these calculations, all we have done is convert masses to moles or vice versa.

(4) Make use of formulae or chemical equations.

(a) Formulae. What is the concentration of hydroxide ion in a 0.5 mol dm⁻³ solution of $Ba(OH)_2$?

Each barium hydroxide contains two hydroxide ions.
Thus concentration of OH^- = 2 × concentration of $Ba(OH)_2$
= 2 × 0.5 mol dm⁻³
= 1.0 mol dm⁻³

16

(b) <u>Acid-base equations</u>. What amount of sulphuric acid is completely neutralised by 0.2 mol of sodium hydroxide? The formulae in the equation are best read in terms of moles of compound.

$$\text{e.g. } H_2SO_4 + 2NaOH \rightarrow Na_2SO_4 + 2H_2O$$

reads: one mole of sulphuric acid reacts with two moles of sodium hydroxide to give one mole of sodium sulphate and two moles of water.

Hence 0.2 mol of sodium hydroxide exactly neutralise 0.1 mol of sulphuric acid (check with equation - should your answer be larger or smaller?).

(c) <u>Redox equations</u>. What amount of manganate(VII) ion is completely neutralised by 0.25 mol of ethanedioate ion?

In this example the equation is best written in terms of ions:

$$2MnO_4^-(aq) + 5C_2O_4^{2-}(aq) + 16H^+(aq) \rightarrow 2Mn^{2+}(aq) + 10CO_2(g) + 8H_2O(l)$$

This reads as two moles of manganate(VII) ion react with 5 moles of ethanedioate ion.

Hence 0.25 mol of ethanedioate ion will react with exactly 2/5 x 0.25 mol of manganate(VII), i.e. 0.10 mol (again, check with equation - should your answer be larger or smaller?).

(5)   <u>Route planning - volumetric calculations</u>.

Write down the balanced equation for the reaction.

Underneath the equation, write down all the information you are given and note (e.g. with a question mark) what you need to find.

e.g. H_2SO_4 + $2NaOH \rightarrow Na_2SO_4 + 2H_2O$

	(3)
	←
20 cm^3	25 cm^3
↓ (4)	↑ (2)
? mol dm^{-3}	? mol dm^{-3}
	↑ (1)
	4.00 g dm^{-3}

where:

(1)   the point to start: the concentration of sodium hydroxide may be found from its concentration in g dm^{-3} and M_r,

(2)   the amount in moles of sodium hydroxide may be found from the volume and concentration,

(3)   the amount of sulphuric acid in moles may be found from the amount of sodium hydroxide,

(4)   the last step: the amount and volume of sulphuric acid leads to its concentration.

3.3 ACID/BASE TITRATIONS.

3.3.1 THE CONCENTRATION OF ETHANOIC ACID IN VINEGAR.
The ethanoic (acetic) acid present in vinegar may be titrated against a standard solution of alkali. The acid content of different brands of vinegar may also be compared to decide on the "best buy".

ASSESSMENT: Refer to the guidance given in the introduction on manipulative skills (1.7), use of volumetric apparatus (2.3) and on calculations (1.5). Help is given in section 3.2 of this topic on the interpretation of the results of titrations.

PROCEDURE:

(1) The vinegar must first be diluted to a suitable concentration for titration against 0.100 mol dm^{-3} sodium hydroxide. This also reduces the intensity of the vinegar colour sufficiently for the indicator colour to be seen. Pipette 25.0 cm^3 of the vinegar into a 250 cm^3 volumetric flask. Make up to the mark with distilled water. The solution is best mixed by pouring into a clean, dry beaker.

(2) Pipette 25.0 cm^3 of this diluted vinegar into a 250 cm^3 conical flask. Add a drop of phenolphthalein indicator. This indicator is colourless in acid and deep pink in alkali.

(3) Fill your burette with the standard solution of alkali. Titrate the vinegar in the conical flask with this alkali. The end-point is reached when the mixture in the flask just turns pink.

(4) Repeat the titration until you have a consistent result. You should make a copy of Table 1 in which to record your results.

Name: Date:

Burette Readings/cm^3	Trial	Accurate		
	I	II	III	
Second				
First				
Volume taken				

SUMMARY:
25.0 cm^3 of the diluted vinegar required .... cm^3 of 0.100 mol dm^{-3} sodium hydroxide for exact neutralisation.

Table 1: Titration of Diluted Vinegar against Standard Sodium Hydroxide.

QUESTIONS:

(1) The formula of ethanoic acid is CH_3CO_2H. It is a monobasic acid, the acidic hydrogen being the one attached to an oxygen atom. Write the equation for its reaction with sodium hydroxide.

(2) From the volume of alkali used in the titration, calculate the amount, in moles, of sodium hydroxide needed.

(3) Hence what is the amount, in moles, of ethanoic acid in the 25.0 cm^3 sample of diluted vinegar?

(4) Calculate the concentration, in mol dm^{-3}, of ethanoic acid in the diluted vinegar.

(5) Calculate the concentration, in mol dm^{-3}, of acid in the original vinegar.

(6) Calculate the mass concentration, in g dm^{-3}, of acid in the original vinegar.

(7) If more than one sample of vinegar has been used in your group, you can compare their relative value for money if you know the purchase prices.

3.3.2 DETERMINATION OF THE NUMBER OF MOLES OF WATER OF CRYSTALLISATION IN A BORATE.

Sodium or potassium borate may be used for this determination. They do not have the same number of moles of water of crystallisation present.

Borate ions are basic and are neutralised by acid:

$$B_4O_7^{2-}(aq) + 2H^+(aq) + 5H_2O \rightarrow 4H_3BO_3(aq)$$

The product is a weak acid, boric acid.

ASSESSMENT: Refer to the guidance given in the introduction on manipulative skills (1.7), use of volumetric apparatus (2.3) and on calculations (1.5). Help is given in section 3.2 of this topic on the interpretation of the results of titrations.

PROCEDURE:

(1) Pipette 25.0 cm^3 of the borate solution provided into a 250 cm^3 conical flask.

(2) Titrate against the standardised 0.100 mol dm^{-3} hydrochloric acid provided. The indicator to use is screened methyl orange. This is green in alkali, purple in acid and grey to almost colourless at the end point. Use one small drop only.

(3) Repeat the titration as many times as you think necessary to achieve accurate results.

(4) Make a copy of Table 2 in which to record your results.

Name: Date:

Burette Readings/cm^3	Trial		Accurate	
		I	II	III
Second				
First				
Volume taken				

SUMMARY:
Hence 25.0 cm^3 of the borate solution requires .... cm^3 of 0.100 mol dm^{-3}
hydrochloric acid for exact neutralisation.
Your teacher will give you the following information:
The mass concentration of the borate was .... g dm^{-3}.
The salt used contained the ....cation.

Table 2: Titration of Borate against Hydrochloric Acid.

QUESTIONS:

(1) Calculate the amount, in moles, of hydrochloric acid used.

(2) Hence find the amount, in moles, of borate ion in your 25.0 cm^3 sample.

(3) From this calculate the concentration of the borate in mol dm^{-3}.

(4) Use this concentration in mol dm^{-3} and the concentration of the borate in g dm^{-3} (given to you by your teacher) to find the relative molecular mass of the salt.

(5) The general formula of the salt is $M_2B_4O_7$, where M = Na or K. Use this formula and the relative molecular mass you have just calculated to find the mass of water in the salt. Hence find the moles of water of crystallisation present.

(6) Write out the formula of the hydrated crystals.

3.3.3 THE EFFLORESCENCE OF WASHING SODA CRYSTALS.

When hydrated sodium carbonate, $Na_2CO_3.10H_2O$ (washing soda), is left exposed to the air it becomes white and powdery. This is because it loses water of crystallisation, a process known as efflorescence.

The sample of washing soda provided has lost some water of crystallisation. Plan an experiment to determine the percentage loss of water of crystallisation. You are provided with apparatus usually available in the laboratory, including an accurate balance and volumetric glassware. Apart from your washing soda crystals, you have an adequate supply of standardised 0.100 mol dm^{-3} hydrochloric acid and the indicator screened methyl orange. You may use your practical notes and any text book.

ASSESSMENT: Refer to the guidelines on planning exercises (1.6) in the introduction. In your plan you must include details of the following:

(1) any masses to be weighed (show any calculations used to decide these weighings),

(2) clear instructions on your method,

(3) a table in which results may be recorded,

(4) (if you carry out your suggested method) the calculation to find the percentage loss of water of crystallisation.

You do NOT need to give details of burette or pipette technique. You may find the section on titration calculations helpful.

3.3.4 A TITRATION WITH TWO INDICATORS.

The sodium carbonate is put in the titration flask and phenolphthalein is added. It is then titrated against the acid until the pink colour just disappears and a first end point is found. Addition of screened methyl orange at this stage gives a green colour. Continued titration of the same sample against the acid enables a second end point to be found.

The two titration results may be used to write two stepwise equations of the reactions involved. Indicator theory may be used to explain why the two indicators give different end points.

ASSESSMENT: Refer to the guidance given in the introduction on manipulative skills (1.7), use of volumetric apparatus (2.3) and on calculations (1.5). Help is given in section 3.2 of this topic on the interpretation of the results of titrations.

PROCEDURE:

(1) Pipette 25.0 cm^3 of the 0.05 mol dm^{-3} sodium carbonate provided into a 250 cm^3 conical flask. Add a drop of phenolphthalein indicator.

(2) Titrate against the standardised 0.100 mol dm^{-3} hydrochloric acid provided until the pink colour just disappears. Record the volume of acid used.

(3) Now add one drop of screened methyl orange indicator to the contents of the conical flask and continue the titration until another end point is found. Record this second volume of acid used.

(4) Wash out the conical flask and repeat the two stages with further 25.0 cm^3 aliquots of the sodium carbonate to obtain consistent results.

Make a copy of Table 3 for your results.

Name: Date:

Burette Readings/cm^3	Trial		Accurate	
		I	II	III
Second*				
First				
Volume at first end point (with phenolphthalein)				
Third				
Second*				
Volume at second end point (with screened methyl orange)				

* Note that the second burette reading is recorded twice in the table.

SUMMARY:
Therefore 25.0 cm^3 of 0.05 mol dm^{-3} sodium carbonate requires........cm^3 of 0.100 mol dm^{-3} hydrochloric acid at the first end point and a further .... cm^3 at the second end point.

Table 3: Sodium Carbonate against Hydrochloric Acid using Two Indicators.

QUESTIONS:

(1) Calculate the amount, in moles, of sodium carbonate taken.

(2) Calculate the amount, in moles, of hydrochloric acid needed at the first end point with phenolphthalein indicator.

(3) Hence determine the mole ratio of sodium carbonate reacting with hydrochloric acid at this end point.

(4) Bearing in mind that sodium carbonate is the salt of a weak, dibasic acid, can you make any suggestions regarding the formulae of the products formed when carbonate and acid react together in this mole ratio?

(5) Write an equation for the reaction at the first end point.

(6) Calculate the amount, in moles, of hydrochloric acid needed at the second end point. Express this as a mole ratio to the original amount of sodium carbonate taken.

(7) Now write an equation for the reaction at the second end point. remember that this is the reaction of hydrochloric acid with the products of the first reaction.

(8) Look up the pK_{In} values of the two indicators in your Data Book. Explain why they enable two different end points to be found.

3.4 REDOX TITRATIONS

3.4.1 THE EQUATION FOR THE REACTION OF IODATE(V) WITH IODIDE.

Iodine may be titrated against standard sodium thiosulphate using starch as an indicator. The starch gives a deep blue colour and the end point is reached when the solution just turns colourless. The reaction between thiosulphate ions and iodine is

$$2S_2O_3^{2-}(aq) + I_2(aq) \rightarrow S_4O_6^{2-}(aq) + 2I^-(aq)$$

When an acidified solution of iodate(V) is treated with an excess of iodide, iodine is liberated. The solution must contain an excess of hydrogen ions to combine with the oxygen atoms attached to the iodate(V) ions and form water.

This may be determined by titration against standard sodium thiosulphate.

If the original concentration of the iodate(V) is known, the equation for the reaction of iodate(V) with iodide may then be found.

ASSESSMENT: Refer to the guidance given in the introduction on manipulative skills (1.7), use of volumetric apparatus (2.3) and on calculations (1.5). Help is given in section 3.2 of this topic on the interpretation of the results of titrations.

PROCEDURE:

(1) Pipette 10.0 cm^3 of the potassium iodate, KIO_3, solution provided into a 250 cm^3 conical flask.

(2) Add about 10 cm^3 of dilute sulphuric acid followed by about 20 cm^3 of the aqueous potassium iodide, KI.

(3) The liberated iodine is then titrated against the 0.050 mol dm^{-3} sodium thiosulphate. The starch indicator must not be added until the iodine colour has been nearly removed by the thiosulphate. Add about 1 cm^3 of indicator when the solution in the flask is pale yellow.

(4) Titrate until the blue colour just disappears.

(5) Repeat the titration as many times as you think necessary to achieve accurate results.

(6) Make a copy of Table 4 for your results.

QUESTIONS:

(1) Calculate the amount, in moles, of thiosulphate ion used in the titration.

(2) Hence determine the amount, in moles, of iodine molecules, I_2, liberated by the iodate(V).

Name: Date:

| Burette readings/cm^3 | Trial | | Accurate | |
		I	II	III
Second				
First				
Volume taken				

SUMMARY:
The iodine liberated when 10.0 cm^3 of potassium iodate(V) are treated with an excess of potassium iodide and sulphuric acid reacts with exactly .... cm^3 of 0.050 mol dm^{-3} sodium thiosulphate.

Table 4: The Titration of Iodine from the Iodate(V)/Iodide Reaction.

(3) The concentration of the potassium iodate(V) was 3.00 g dm^{-3}. How many moles of iodate(V) ions are present in 10.0 cm^3 of this solution?

(4) What is the mole ratio of iodate(V) taken to iodine molecules formed?

(5) Write a balanced ionic equation for the reaction of iodate(V) with acidified iodide ions.

3.4.2 DETERMINATION OF SODIUM CHLORATE(I) IN BLEACH.
Most of the bleaching properties of domestic bleach are due to the presence of the chlorate(I) (hypochlorite) ion, ClO$^-$. The concentration of this ion may be found by adding an excess of potassium iodide, acidifying, and titrating the liberated iodine against standard sodium thiosulphate solution.

The chlorate(I) content of a number of different brands may be compared using this method in order to find the best buy. Use of the thick bleaches is best avoided as they give difficulty with the end point.

ASSESSMENT: Refer to the guidance given in the introduction on manipulative skills (1.7), use of volumetric apparatus (2.3) and on calculations (1.5). Help is given in section 3.2 of this topic on the interpretation of the results of titrations.

PROCEDURE:

(1) Pipette 10.0 cm^3 of the commercial bleach into a 250 cm^3 volumetric flask. Add distilled water to make up to the mark. Mix well. Most commercial bleach contains small amounts of detergent to improve its wetting properties so it is inadvisable to shake the solution vigorously.

(2) Pipette 10.0 cm^3 of your diluted bleach into a 100 cm^3 conical flask.

(3) Add about 10 cm^3 of the potassium iodide solution provided, followed by about 10 cm^3 of dilute sulphuric acid.

(4) Titrate the mixture against the standard 0.025 mol dm^{-3} sodium thiosulphate solution provided, adding about 1 cm^3 of starch indicator when the solution has become pale yellow. The end point is reached when the blue colour disappears.

(5) Repeat the titration until you have sufficient consistent results. Record your results in a suitable fashion.

QUESTIONS:

(1) Balance the following equation for the reaction of chlorate(I) with iodide:

$$ClO^- + I^- + H^+ \rightarrow Cl^- + I_2 + H_2O$$

(2) Write the equation for the reaction of thiosulphate with iodine.

(3) Why is it inadvisable to add acid to your diluted bleach before adding the iodide?

(4) From your titration results, calculate the amount, in moles, of thiosulphate ion required.

(5) Hence find the amount of iodine molecules, I_2, present.

(6) From this figure, calculate the amount of chlorate(I) in your diluted 10.0 cm^3 sample.

(7) Determine the concentration, in mol dm^{-3}, of your diluted bleach.

(8) What is the concentration of the undiluted bleach?

(9) If several different brands have been have been used in your group you can compare their relative value for money if you know their purchase prices.

3.4.3 THE STANDARDISATION OF POTASSIUM MANGANATE(VII).

Potassium manganate(VII) can be difficult to dissolve completely in water. It is intensely coloured and it is not easy to see undissolved crystals. Also it slowly decomposes in water to manganese(IV) oxide. This oxide is often seen as a brown stain on the walls of glass containers which have contained the solution for some time.

For these reasons it is necessary to standardise solutions of potassium manganate(VII). A suitable reagent is ethanedioic acid or one of its soluble salts. The redox reaction with the ethanedioate ion is slow at room temperature but rapid at about 60 °C. The titration is thus carried out using a hot solution.

You will make up your own solution of potassium manganate(VII) to standardise. Having standardised your solution, you will use it in the next experiment to determine the percentage oxidation of a sample of aqueous iron(II) sulphate.

ASSESSMENT: Refer to the guidance given in the introduction on manipulative skills (1.7), use of volumetric apparatus (2.3) and on calculations (1.5). Help is given in section 3.2 of this topic on the interpretation of the results of titrations.

PROCEDURE:

(1) First make up your solution of potassium manganate(VII). Weigh accurately about 0.75 g of solid potassium manganate(VII).

(2) Add about 25 cm^3 of distilled water to the crystals in a small beaker. Make sure you wash the crystals from the weighing bottle into this beaker. Transfer this solution to a 250 cm^3 volumetric flask, washing the beaker thoroughly and transferring the washings into the flask. Make up to 250 cm^3 with distilled water and mix the solution thoroughly. Place on one side until needed.

(3) Pipette 25.0 cm^3 of the 0.05 mol dm^{-3} sodium ethanedioate provided into a 250 cm^3 conical flask.

(4) Acidify this solution with 25 cm^3 of dilute sulphuric acid.

(5) Heat the flask over a bunsen, on a tripod, until it is just too hot to hold your hand against it. It is better not to use a thermometer as solution may be lost on removal of the thermometer.

(6) Fill the burette with the potassium manganate(VII) solution and titrate the contents of the flask. The mixture will cool during the titration, so be ready to heat it up again.

(7) At first there is a delay before any reaction is seen, then the manganate(VII) turns colourless. Further additions are decolorised immediately.

(8) The end point is reached when the solution just turns pink. The intense colour of the manganate(VII) ion makes it difficult to read the bottom of the meniscus. For this solution only, take readings using the top of the meniscus.

(9) Repeat the titration as many times as you think necessary to achieve accurate results. If a solution goes cloudy during a titration, discard this mixture and carry out a fresh titration.

(10) Record your results in a suitable manner.

QUESTIONS:

(1) Calculate the amount of ethanedioate ions present in 25.0 cm^3 of the 0.05 mol dm^{-3} sodium ethanedioate, $Na_2C_2O_4$.

(2) The ethanedioate is oxidised by the manganate(VII) ion in the acid solution to carbon dioxide. Write a balanced ionic equation for the reaction.

(3) Now calculate the amount of manganate(VII) ion needed to react exactly with the ethanedioate ion.

(4) From your titration volume, and your answer to (3), calculate the concentration of manganate(VII) in mol dm^{-3}.

(5) Hence find the concentration of potassium manganate(VII) in g dm^{-3}.

(6) From your answer to (5), calculate the mass of potassium manganate(VII) dissolved in your volumetric flask. Compare this mass to your weighing. Explain any difference in the two masses.

(7) Can you suggest any reason for the delay seen when the manganate(VII) is first added to the hot, acidified ethanedioate?

3.4.4 THE AERIAL OXIDATION OF AQUEOUS IRON(II) SULPHATE.
The concentration of iron(II) in a solution may be determined by titration against potassium manganate(VII). If the original concentration of the iron(II) is also known, the percentage oxidation of the solution by the air may be calculated.

The solution of iron(II) provided was made by dissolving 30.0 g of hydrated iron(II) sulphate, $FeSO_4.7H_2O$, in water, leaving it to stand for several days, and then making up to one cubic decimetre.

ASSESSMENT: Refer to the guidance given in the introduction on manipulative skills (1.7), use of volumetric apparatus (2.3) and on calculations (1.5). Help is given in section 3.2 of this topic on the interpretation of the results of titrations.

PROCEDURE:

(1) Pipette 25 cm^3 of the partly oxidised iron(II) solution provided into a 250 cm^3 conical flask.

(2) Acidify this solution with about 25 cm^3 of dilute sulphuric acid.

(3) Titrate the mixture against the standardised potassium manganate(VII) solution provided. The end point is reached when the solution just turns pink.

(4) Repeat the titration until you have sufficient results. Record your results in the way that you have been shown.

QUESTIONS:

(1) The manganese containing product of the reaction is the Mn^{2+}(aq) ion. This is colourless in solution. What is the oxidation number of iron in the product? What is the colour of this ion?

(2) Why is it necessary to use acid in this titration?

(3) Write a balanced ionic equation for the reaction of manganate(VII) with iron(II) in acid solution.

(4) From your titration result determine the amount, in moles, of manganate(VII) ion used. Remember to use the concentration that you found for the manganate(VII) solution in the standardisation experiment.

(5) Use this figure and the equation for the reaction to calculate the amount of iron(II) present in your 25 cm^3 sample of solution.

(6) Next calculate the concentration of iron(II) ions in mol dm^{-3}.

(7) The original iron(II) solution was made using 30.0 g dm^{-3} of hydrated iron(II) sulphate. Calculate the concentration of iron(II) ions in the original solution.

(8) What is the percentage of the iron(II) which has been oxidised?

4. QUALITATIVE INORGANIC TESTS

4.1 Introduction to qualitative inorganic tests.
4.2 Identification of gases.
4.3 Tests on anions in solution.
4.4 Tests on cations in solution.
4.5 Tests for oxidising and reducing agents.
4.6 Inorganic exercise A.
4.7 Inorganic exercise B.
4.8 Inorganic exercise C.

4.1 INTRODUCTION TO QUALITATIVE INORGANIC TESTS.

AIMS: This section serves to consolidate and extend the many simple test tube reactions involving inorganic cations, anions and gases that you met on your Chemistry course before A-level. You will learn to use the results of such tests to arrive at deductions concerning the composition of unknown inorganic substances.

THEORY: Traditionally, qualitative inorganic analysis was taught as part of A-level Chemistry. This involved the systematic application of a sequence of tests to an unknown substance. The sequence of tests was designed to narrow down methodically the choice of possible ions present until a definite identification of the substance could be made. Whilst thorough, the process is somewhat mechanical, allowing little scope for independent thought.

Nowadays, you are presented with an unknown substance and a series of tests to perform on the substance. These tests are carefully chosen to provide a number of clues as to the identity of the substance. You then use these clues to make a reasoned identification of the substance, rather in the manner of a detective solving a crime.

In this topic you are first introduced to tests that are characteristic of individual anions and cations. During these tests you will need to identify a number of gases. Section 4.2 provides a summary of the properties that enable these gases to be identified. Remember, cations carry a positive electric charge, anions a negative electric charge!

The ions with which you will become familiar are: NH_4^+, Mg^{2+}, Al^{3+}, Ca^{2+}, Cr^{2+}, Mn^{2+}, Fe^{2+}, Fe^{3+}, Ni^{2+}, Cu^{2+}, Zn^{2+}, Ba^{2+}, Pb^{2+}, Ag^+, CO_3^{2-}, NO_3^-, NO_2^-, S^{2-}, SO_4^{2-}, SO_3^{2-}, $S_2O_3^{2-}$, Cl^-, Br^-, I^- and CrO_4^{2-}.

Gases you should be able to recognise are: ammonia, carbon dioxide, carbon monoxide, hydrogen sulphide, sulphur dioxide, nitrogen(IV) oxide, hydrogen chloride, hydrogen bromide, hydrogen iodide, chlorine, bromine, iodine, nitrogen, oxygen, hydrogen and water vapour. Organic gases that you will meet later in this text include methane and ethene. You will find that most organic compounds have characteristic odours which you should endeavour to recognise.

Redox reactions can also be useful in making an identification. You are introduced to those which are more useful before being given some unknown substances to identify.

SUMMARY: At the end of this topic you should

(1) be familiar with the properties and special tests that enable gases to be identified (see list above),

(2) know the tests and observations that are characteristic of the anions listed above,

(3) know the observations and deductions that may be made when solutions of cations are treated with aqueous sodium hydroxide or aqueous ammonia,

(4) be able to recognise the presence of an oxidising or reducing agent by use of appropriate tests,

(5) be able to make deductions from the observations made during a series of tests and use these deductions to identify an unknown substance or to make a more general conclusion about a substance.

LINKS: Many of the reactions in this topic appear in topics 10 to 16 of this text. Hence this topic and the topics 10 to 16 provide you with a wide range of experience of inorganic chemistry. The reactions met in these topics will considerably help your learning of inorganic chemistry. Redox reactions are also studied in Topic 8 and are used in many of the titration exercises in Topic 3.

4.2 IDENTIFICATION OF GASES.

HAZARD WARNINGS: *MANY GASES ARE VERY POISONOUS, SOME FORM EXPLOSIVE MIXTURES WITH AIR. REACTIONS INVOLVING TOXIC GASES SHOULD ALWAYS BE CARRIED OUT IN AN EFFICIENT FUME CUPBOARD.*

This section is intended for your reference whenever you wish to identify a gas. You will not meet all of the gases in this topic, some you will meet in topics 10 to 16 and a few in topics 17 to 22 of this text. Some elements and compounds are not gases at room temperature but have been included as they are volatile and may appear as gases when reaction mixtures are warmed.

When a gas is evolved you should always record its
COLOUR
ODOUR
ACTION ON DAMP LITMUS (pink and blue)
ACTION ON A LIGHTED SPLINT.

These four observations will give a good indication of the identity of the gas:

COLOUR:	coloured gases	- chlorine (pale yellow-green) - bromine (orange-red) - iodine (violet) - nitrogen(IV) oxide (brown) (N.B. bromine is a dark red liquid and iodine a lustrous black solid at room temperature.)
	colourless gases	- all others on the list in section 4.1. However, some of these give misty (white) fumes in moist air. These are the hydrogen halides and water vapour.
ODOUR:	bleach	- chlorine, bromine, iodine or nitrogen(IV) oxide
	acidic	- hydrogen chloride, bromide or iodide, sulphur dioxide, ethanoic acid vapour
	pungent	- ammonia, ethene
	bad eggs	- hydrogen sulphide
	sweet	- a number of volatile organic compounds
	odourless	- carbon dioxide, carbon monoxide, hydrogen, water vapour, nitrogen or oxygen.

LITMUS: blue turns pink   - acid gas - sulphur dioxide, hydrogen
                                    chloride, bromide or iodide, nitrogen(IV)
                                    oxide, chlorine, bromine or iodine,
                                    carbon dioxide, hydrogen sulphide

           pink turns blue   - ammonia
           bleached   - chlorine, other halogens, nitrogen(IV)
                                    oxide (very slowly).

SPLINT: gas burns   - hydrogen (with a squeaky pop or orange-blue
                                    flame)
                                  - hydrogen sulphide
                                  - carbon monoxide (with a flickering blue flame)
                                  - methane, ethene, other hydrocarbon or volatile
                                    organic compound (yellow flame)

           splint put out   - carbon dioxide, sulphur dioxide, hydrogen
                                    chloride, bromide, iodide, water vapour or
                                    ammonia.

Then confirm gas by a special test:

ammonia   - only alkaline gas that you will meet,
                                   turns pink litmus blue.
carbon monoxide   - blue flickering flame (not conclusive)
carbon dioxide   - bubble through lime water which turns milky
sulphur dioxide   - a drop of aqueous potassium dichromate on filter
                                   paper is turned from orange to green
hydrogen sulphide   - damp lead ethanoate paper is turned silvery
                                   black
hydrogen   - burns with a squeaky pop
oxygen   - a glowing splint relights or glows more
                                   brightly
hydrogen chloride,   - all produce dense white fumes when brought
hydrogen bromide,   into contact with a drop of aqueous ammonia on
hydrogen iodide   a glass rod
chlorine,   - all four are oxidising agents and turn damp
bromine,   starch-iodide paper blue-black (identify by
iodine,   colour and effect on damp blue litmus paper)
nitrogen(IV) oxide
water vapour   - blue cobalt chloride paper turns pink

N.B. See subsection 2.2.4 for techniques for testing gases.

4.3 TESTS ON ANIONS IN SOLUTION.

HAZARD WARNING: *THE TESTS ON SULPHITE, SULPHIDE AND NITRITE IONS*
                       PRODUCE TOXIC GASES.

In this practical you are introduced to the tests which help identify aqueous solutions of anions. Gases are produced in some of these tests. They should be identified by their colour, odour, action on litmus paper, action on a lighted splint and (where appropriate) by means of a special test (see section 4.2 above).

ASSESSMENT: You may be assessed on your manipulative skills (see 1.7 and 2.2) and on your observations (see 1.2).

PROCEDURE: You will need a copy of Table 1 from the Teachers' Guide. Carry out the tests described. Note any colour changes and the formation and colour of any precipitates, and identify any gases evolved. Start by treating about 2 cm^3 of each of the anion solutions with about 2 cm^3 of dilute hydrochloric acid. If there is no reaction with cold acid, warm the mixture. Then try the other tests.

29

4.4 TESTS ON CATIONS IN SOLUTION.

In this practical you are provided with solutions containing cations as chloride, sulphate or nitrate salts. The solutions are labelled A to M and you are required to identify the cation present in each solution.

ASSESSMENT: You may be assessed on your manipulative skills (see 1.7 and 2.2) and on your deductions (see 1.4).

PROCEDURE:

(1) Put about 2 cm^3 of solution A in a test tube and add dilute aqueous sodium hydroxide dropwise until there is no further change. Now warm the mixture gently and then boil (take care, the mixture may "bump" if a precipitate is present).

(2) Repeat the test using aqueous ammonia (ammonium hydroxide) in place of the sodium hydroxide but do not warm the mixture.

(3) Use Tables 5 and 6 below to identify the cation in solution A.

(4) Record your observations and deductions in a tabular form.

(5) Repeat the steps (1) to (4) with each of the remaining solutions B to M, in turn. In a few cases a complete identification of the cation is not possible. One solution contains two cations.

4.5 TESTS FOR OXIDISING AND REDUCING AGENTS.

In this exercise you will investigate a few reactions which help establish the presence of an oxidising or a reducing agent.

ASSESSMENT: You may be assessed on your manipulative skills (see 1.7 and 2.2) and on your deductions (see 1.4).

PROCEDURE: Carry out the test tube reactions described in Table 2 from the Teachers' Guide and then answer the questions that follow. Three oxidising agents are first treated with aqueous potassium iodide. Three reducing agents are then treated with acidified aqueous potassium manganate(VII). Finally two reducing agents are treated with aqueous iodine.

When you have finished the tests answer the following questions:

(1) Name the coloured product seen when the oxidising agents acted on the aqueous potassium iodide. What test could you carry out to help confirm this product?

(2) What is the general effect of reducing agents on the colour of acidified potassium manganate(VII)? What is the manganate(VII) ion reduced to?

(3) What is the general effect of reducing agents on the colour of aqueous iodine? What is the iodine reduced to?

(4) Write balanced ionic equations for the above reactions. Underneath your equations write the oxidation numbers of the elements present and show clearly which is oxidised and which is reduced.

OBSERVATION	DEDUCTION	PRODUCT
NO PRECIPITATE FORMED: 1. No precipitate formed but a pungent gas evolved on warming which turns pink litmus blue.	NH_4^+ present.	Gas is ammonia.
2. No apparent change.	Na^+ or K^+. (Ca^{2+} or Ba^{2+} if original solution too dilute.)	
COLOURLESS SOLUTION PRODUCING: 3. a white precipitate which is insoluble in excess alkali.	Mg^{2+}, Ca^{2+} or Ba^{2+} present.	Metal hydroxide precipitated.
4. white precipitate which is soluble in excess alkali.	Pb^{2+}, Al^{3+} or Zn^{2+} present.	Precipitate of metal hydroxide dissolves to give PbO_2^{2-}, ZnO_2^{2-} or AlO_2^-.
5. white precipitate which turns pale brown (may miss white stage).	Mn^{2+} present.	Precipitate of $Mn(OH)_2$ oxidised by air to Mn(III).
6. grey-brown precipitate.	Ag^+ present.	Precipitate is silver(I) oxide.
7. dirty green precipitate which slowly turns rust coloured at the surface.	Fe^{2+} present.	Precipitate of $Fe(OH)_2$ oxidised by air to Fe(III).
COLOURED SOLUTION: 8. rust coloured precipitate from a yellow solution.	Fe^{3+} present.	Precipitate of $Fe(OH)_3$.
9. Blue or green solution producing: a) a pale blue precipitate which turns black on heating.	Cu^{2+} present.	Precipitate of $Cu(OH)_2$ dehydrated to black CuO.
b) a pale green precipitate, insoluble in excess alkali.	Ni^{2+} present.	$Ni(OH)_2$ is precipitated.
c) a grey-green precipitate which is soluble in excess alkali (may not appear if original solution is too dilute).	Cr^{3+} present.	$Cr(OH)_3$ is precipitated, dissolves to give CrO_2^-.

Table 5: 4.4 Reactions of Cations in Solution with Sodium Hydroxide.

OBSERVATION	DEDUCTION	PRODUCT
NO APPARENT CHANGE.	Na^+, K^+, NH_4^+, Ca^{2+} or Ba^{2+}.	
COLOURLESS SOLUTION PRODUCING A: 1. white precipitate which is insoluble in excess alkali.	Mg^{2+}, Pb^{2+} or Al^{3+} present.	Metal hydroxide precipitated.
2. white precipitate which is soluble in excess alkali.	Zn^{2+} present.	Precipitate of metal hydroxide dissolves to give $[Zn(NH_3)_4]^{2+}$.
3. white precipitate which turns pale brown (may miss white stage).	Mn^{2+} present.	Precipitate of $Mn(OH)_2$ oxidised by air to Mn(III).
4. grey-brown precipitate which dissolves in excess alkali to give a colourless solution.	Ag^+ present.	Precipitate is silver(I) oxide. Dissolves to give $[Ag(NH_3)_2]^+$.
5. dirty green precipitate which slowly turns rust coloured at the surface.	Fe^{2+} present.	Precipitate of $Fe(OH)_2$ oxidised by air to Fe(III).
COLOURED SOLUTION: 6. Yellow solution producing a rust coloured precipitate.	Fe^{3+} present.	Precipitate of $Fe(OH)_3$.
7. Blue or green solution producing:		
a) a pale blue precipitate which dissolves to give a royal blue solution in excess alkali.	Cu^{2+} present.	Precipitate of $Cu(OH)_2$ dissolves to give $[Cu(NH_3)_4]^{2+}$.
b) a pale green precipitate which dissolves to give a blue solution in excess alkali.	Ni^{2+} present.	$Ni(OH)_2$ precipitate dissolves to give $[Ni(NH_3)_6]^{2+}$.
c) a grey-green precipitate.	Cr^{3+} present.	$Cr(OH)_3$ is precipitated.

Table 6: 4.4 Reactions of Cations in Solution with Ammonium Hydroxide.

4.6 INORGANIC EXERCISE A.

You are provided with a solution, A, which contains one cation and two anions. Carry out the tests described in Table 3 from the Teachers' Guide and use your deductions to identify the ions present.

ASSESSMENT: You may be assessed on your manipulative skills (see 1.7 and 2.2), on your observations (1.2) or on your deductions (1.4).

PROCEDURE: Carry out the test tube experiments shown in Table 3 from the Teachers' Guide with solution A. In all tests, the reagent should be added gradually until no further change is observed. Record your observations and your deductions in the spaces provided. Identify the cation and two anions present in A. Your observations should include details of colour changes, precipitates and tests on gases evolved. You should indicate clearly at what stage in a test a change occurs. Credit will only be given for those tests specified and for tests to identify gases.

4.7 INORGANIC EXERCISE B.

Solution B contains a salt having two cations and one anion. Carry out the tests specified and record your observations and deductions in the spaces provided. Not all of your observations will lead to a deduction. Use a copy of Table 4 from the Teachers' Guide.

ASSESSMENT: You may be assessed on your manipulative skills (see 1.7 and 2.2), on your observations (1.2) or on your deductions (1.4).

4.8 INORGANIC EXERCISE C.

You are provided with solution C1 (which contains a salt having one cation and one anion) and solid C2. Carry out the tests specified and record your observations and deductions in the spaces provided. Not all of your observations will lead to a deduction. Use a copy of Table 5 from the Teachers' Guide.

ASSESSMENT: You may be assessed on your manipulative skills (see 1.7 and 2.2), on your observations (1.2) or on your deductions (1.4).

When you have finished the tests answer the following questions:

(1)   What is the cation present in solution C1?

(2)   Deduce what you can about the nature of the anion in solution C1, giving your reasons.

(3)   Deduce what you can about the nature of solid C2, giving your reasons.

(4)   Name the final precipitate obtained in test 3(ii).

5. RELATIVE MASSES OF ATOMS AND MOLECULES

5.1 Introduction.
5.2 Determination of the relative atomic mass of copper.
5.3 Determination of the relative molecular masses of gases.
5.4 Determination of the relative molecular mass of a volatile liquid.

5.1 INTRODUCTION.

AIMS: These experiments introduce you to some ways in which relative masses of atoms and molecules may be found. The experiments involving gases and volatile liquids are derived from classical methods. The topic will give you practice at calculations involving the Ideal Gas Equation and electrolysis as well as finding relative atomic and molecular masses.

THEORY: Definitions:

The <u>relative atomic mass</u> of an element is defined as the mass of one atom of the element on a scale chosen so that the mass of one atom of the carbon-12 isotope is exactly 12 units.

The <u>relative molecular mass</u> of a compound is defined as the mass of one molecule of the compound on the same scale as that for relative atomic masses.

The <u>mole</u> is the amount of substance of a system which contains as many particles as there are carbon atoms in exactly 12 g of carbon-12. The particles must be specified and may be atoms, molecules, electrons, other particles or specified groups of such particles.

The <u>Avogadro constant</u> is the number of particles in one mole of substance. The particles may be atoms, molecules, ions, electrons etc. The numerical value of the Avogadro constant is 6.02×10^{23}.

<u>Electrolysis</u>: The quantity of electricity passed through a solution is given by:

$$\text{quantity of electricity(couloumbs)} = \text{current(amperes)} \times \text{time(seconds)}.$$

1 mole of electrons = 96,487 coulombs

<u>Ideal Gas Equation</u>: Combination of Boyle's Law and Charles's Law produces the Ideal Gas Equation:

$$pV = nRT$$

where p = pressure, V = volume, n = number of moles, R is the gas constant and T the absolute temperature.

As n = m/M, where m = mass and M = molar mass of gas, the Ideal Gas Equation may be rearranged to give

$$M = mRT/pV$$

It is easiest to use this form of the Ideal Gas Equation as follows. Use S.I. units for volume (cubic metres), pressure (pascals) and temperature (kelvin). With these units the gas constant, $R = 8.31$ J K^{-1} mol^{-1}. Molar mass is usually measured in g mol^{-1}, so grams are used for the unit of mass.

An example will make this clearer. A pure organic liquid of mass 0.146 g produces a vapour occupying a volume of 100 cm^3 at 127 °C and at a pressure of 101 kPa.

100 cm^3 = 100 x 10^{-6} m^3, 127 °C = 400 K and 101 kPa = 1.01 x 10^5 Pa.

Hence M = $\dfrac{0.146 \times 8.31 \times 400}{1.01 \times 10^5 \times 100 \times 10^{-6}}$

= 48 g mol^{-1}

i.e. relative molecular mass of the organic liquid = 48. (Remember relative atomic and molecular masses have no units.)

Correction to s.t.p. The Ideal Gas Equation shows that pV/T = nR, which is constant for a given mass of gas. A volume may be corrected to s.t.p. as in the following example. At 50 °C and 740 mmHg pressure the volume of a gas is 70 cm^3. What is its volume at s.t.p? (i.e 0 °C and 760 mmHg).

pV/T = constant = $\dfrac{760 \times V}{273} = \dfrac{740 \times 70}{273 + 50}$, where V = volume of gas at s.t.p.

i.e. V = $\dfrac{740}{760} \times \dfrac{273}{323} \times 70$ = 57.6 cm^3

SUMMARY: At the end of this topic you should

(1) be able to calculate the quantity of electricity passed during electrolysis,

(2) be able to relate the amount of substance liberated during electrolysis to the amount of electricity passed and the charge on the ions,

(3) be able to correct gas volumes to s.t.p.,

(4) know the experimental methods used for determining the relative molecular masses of gases and volatile liquids,

(5) be able to use the Ideal Gas Equation to calculate relative molecular masses of gases and volatile liquids from measurements of their volume and mass.

LINKS: A knowledge of relative atomic and molecular masses is needed throughout Chemistry. Departure from the Ideal Gas Equation provides evidence for intermolecular forces.

5.2 DETERMINATION OF THE RELATIVE ATOMIC MASS OF COPPER.

In this experiment, aqueous copper sulphate is electrolysed. By finding the mass of copper deposited by the passage of a known quantity of electricity it is possible to determine the relative atomic mass of copper.

ASSESSMENT: refer to the sections on recording results (1.1), weighing (1.7) and on using electrical apparatus (1.7 and 2.10). Guidelines on calculations may be found in section 1.5.

PROCEDURE:

(1) Thoroughly clean two pieces of copper foil using steel wool or fine emery cloth. The foil should be about the size of a microscope slide.

(2) Rinse the pieces of foil thoroughly with distilled water and then propanone. Allow to dry in the air. Handle the foils by the upper ends only and mark these "anode" and "cathode".

(3) Weigh the two foils and record their masses in a suitable table.

(4) Place the foils on opposite sides of a 100 cm^3 beaker and secure them in place by folding the ends over the rim of the beaker. (Alternatively, a microscope slide staining jar may be used. This will enable the foils to be held satisfactorily without folding their ends.)

35

(5) Set up the circuit as shown in figure 4 with the exception of one connection. Use crocodile clips to make the electrical connection to the foils. If these are placed over the folds, they will secure the foils to the beaker. It is important that the foils are secure for the experiment. Take care to connect the anode and cathode correctly!

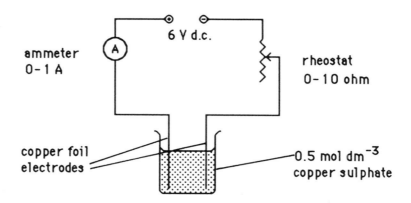

Figure 4: A_r of Copper by Electrolysis.

(6) Three quarters fill the beaker with aqueous copper(II) sulphate. Complete the circuit and adjust the rheostat to give a current of 0.20 A. Start the stopclock at the time you close the switch.

(7) Keep the current constant and allow it to flow for twenty minutes.

(8) Switch off the current at the end of twenty minutes. Remove the electrodes, rinse them with distilled water and then with propanone. Allow them to dry in air.

(9) Now reweigh the electrodes, recording their new masses.

CALCULATION: Answer the following questions:

(1) From the current flowing and time, calculate the quantity of electricity passed through the solution (in coulombs).

(2) Write an ionic equation for the formation of one mole of copper at the cathode.

(3) How many moles of electrons are needed to deposit one mole of copper at the cathode?

(4) From the results obtained in your experiment, calculate the mass of copper that would be deposited on the cathode by one mole of electrons (remember one mole of electrons is 96,487 coulombs).

(5) Hence what is the relative atomic mass of copper?

(6) How does your result compare with that obtained from the mass of copper dissolved from the anode? Look up the data book value for the relative atomic mass of copper.

(7) Can you place limits of quantifiable error on your value? Consider the errors of precision in the measurements you have made (see 2.11).

5.3 DETERMINATION OF THE RELATIVE MOLECULAR MASSES OF GASES.

By finding the mass of a known volume of gas at a given temperature, it is possible to calculate its relative molecular mass using the Ideal Gas Equation.

The weighing of gases in containers causes some difficulty because of the upthrust of air. Traditionally the mass of gas was found by weighing a flask full of gas and then evacuating the flask and reweighing. This is usually difficult in school laboratories.

In order to find the mass of the empty (i.e. evacuated) flask, it is weighed full of air. The density of air and the volume of the flask are then used to calculate the mass of the empty flask. (At s.t.p. the density of air is taken as 1.293 g dm^{-3}, note the units of volume.)

ASSESSMENT: you may be assessed on your skills in handling apparatus and weighing (1.7). If you are being assessed on the interpretation of your results refer to section 1.5.

PROCEDURE:

(1)   Weigh a stoppered 100 cm^3 conical flask to the nearest 0.001 g. Record all your weighings carefully, a tabular presentation may help.

(2)   Insert a gas delivery tube so that the end is very close to the bottom of the flask. Pass the gas through into the flask for about 1-2 minutes to ensure all the air is displaced.

(3)   Remove the delivery tube slowly whilst maintaining the gas flow and replace the stopper. Reweigh the flask.

(4)   Flush the flask again with the same gas and reweigh. Repeat until you are satisfied that there is no significant change in mass between your weighings.

(5)   The gases that you use should be dried by passing them through a U-tube filled with anhydrous calcium chloride. Gases may be obtained from cylinders, appropriate gas generators or the natural gas supply. The latter can give a value close to methane. Your teacher will advise you on sources of gases.

(6)   The volume of the conical flask is found as follows. Mark the position of the bottom of the stopper. Fill the flask with water to this mark and measure the volume of water by pouring it into a measuring cylinder.

(7)   Record the temperature in the laboratory and the atmospheric pressure.

CALCULATION:

(1)   Correct the volume of air to s.t.p.

(2)   From the density of air given above, calculate the mass of air in the flask. Take care with the density and volume units.

(3)   Use this mass of air to find the mass of the flask as though evacuated.

(4)   You can now determine the mass of each gas taken and hence the relative formula masses using the Ideal Gas Equation. (As necessary, convert your volume, pressure and temperature to S.I. units.)

5.4 DETERMINATION OF THE RELATIVE MOLECULAR MASS OF A VOLATILE LIQUID.

The relative molecular mass of a volatile liquid may be found by measuring the volume of vapour formed by a known mass of the liquid at a given temperature and pressure.

In this experiment, a known mass of liquid is vaporised in a gas syringe surrounded by a steam jacket (see figure 5).

ASSESSMENT: refer to the guidelines on calculations (1.5), weighings (1.7) and errors (2.11).

PROCEDURE: (refer to figure 5)

(1)   Draw about 5 cm^3 of air into the large gas syringe and fit the self-sealing rubber cap over the nozzle.

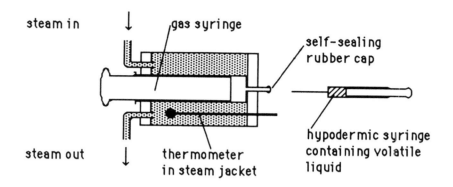

Figure 5: Determination of the M_r of a Volatile Liquid.

(2) Carefully clamp the gas syringe and steam jacket assembly. Pass steam through the steam jacket. When the volume of air in the syringe reaches a steady value and the thermometer reading is also steady, record the volume of air in the syringe and the temperature.

(3) Flush the hypodermic syringe and needle with about 1 cm³ of the volatile liquid provided. Recharge the hypodermic syringe with a further 1 cm³ sample and ensure that no air is present. To do this point the syringe needle up and push the plunger in until a few drops of liquid emerge from the needle. Seal the end of the needle using a small piece of rubber.

(4) Dry the outside of the hypodermic syringe and weigh it. Record this mass.

(5) Remove the rubber from the needle and at once insert the needle through the self-sealing rubber cap on the large gas syringe. Inject about 0.2 cm³ of the liquid into the large syringe, remove the needle from the self-sealing cap and replace the rubber on the end of the needle. Maintain the flow of steam through the steam jacket.

(6) At once reweigh the hypodermic syringe and needle. Record this new mass. Handle the hypodermic needle carefully between weighings to avoid loss of liquid by evaporation or leakage.

(7) Provided the needle is pushed well inside the gas syringe, the liquid injected will evaporate and the plunger of the gas syringe will move out. Record the new volume when the reading has become steady. Check that the temperature has remained steady.

(8) To repeat the experiment, remove the self-sealing cap from the gas syringe and flush the gas syringe several times with air.

(9) Record atmospheric pressure.

CALCULATION:

(1) Find the volume of vapour from the two gas syringe readings and the mass of liquid taken from the two hypodermic syringe weighings.

(2) As necessary convert your pressure, temperature and volume readings to S.I. units.

(3) Substitute your values in the Ideal Gas Equation to find the molar mass of the volatile liquid.

(4) Record your value for the relative molecular mass of the liquid and compare it with the value calculated using the molecular formula and relative atomic masses.

(5) What quantifiable errors can you identify? How will these affect the accuracy of your result? Determine the range of error possible.

6. ENTHALPY CHANGES

6.1 Introduction to enthalpy experiments.
6.2 An illustration of Hess's Law.
6.3 The indirect determination of an enthalpy change.
6.4 The heat of decomposition of calcium carbonate.
6.5 The heat of formation of magnesium oxide.

6.1 INTRODUCTION TO ENTHALPY EXPERIMENTS.

AIMS: This topic will introduce you to simple methods for determining the heat energy (enthalpy) changes of some reactions. The topic also provides much practice at weighing and temperature measurement.

THEORY: Chemists are interested in enthalpy changes for a variety of reasons. In order to design safe chemical plant, a knowledge of the heat energy changes is essential. This enables industrial processes to be designed to be efficient and economic. The small quantity of heat released during a chemical reaction in the laboratory may become dangerously large on the industrial scale. Enthalpy changes also provide us with information regarding the formation or breaking of bonds.

Before you start the practical work in this topic, you should be familiar with the definitions and terminology of thermochemistry. **Remember**:

* An **exothermic** reaction has a **negative enthalpy change** (the sign of ΔH is negative), although the temperature will **rise** during the reaction.

* An **endothermic** reaction has a **positive enthalpy change** (the sign of ΔH is positive), although the temperature will **fall** during the reaction.

Many enthalpy changes cannot be measured directly. For these changes it is necessary to use Hess's Law. A suitable enthalpy cycle involving the enthalpy change required and enthalpy changes which can be measured directly is constructed. Hess's Law is illustrated in 6.2 and applied in 6.3, 6.4 and 6.5.

Hess's Law: The enthalpy change in a chemical reaction is the same regardless of the route by which the change takes place provided the initial and final conditions are the same.

CALCULATIONS: Most of the enthalpy experiments you will carry out in the simplest of apparatus. All reactions will use water as a solvent and your calculations will usually involve working out the heat energy absorbed or released by the water. By using a plastic cup for the reaction mixture, the heat lost to or absorbed from the apparatus may be regarded as negligible. Heat lost to or gained from the surrounding air will also be ignored. Under these experimental conditions it is satisfactory to take the specific heat capacity of water as 4.2 J g^{-1} K^{-1}. Hence for a given volume of aqueous mixture V cm^3 and a temperature change T K, the enthalpy change is given by

enthalpy change = V x 4.2 x T J, since V cm^3 of water has a mass of V g.

Note that the only mass used in this expression is the mass of water as it is only the specific heat capacity of water that is involved.

This enthalpy change is then converted to an enthalpy change per mole by dividing by the number of moles of reagent used and adding a positive or negative sign, as appropriate, to indicate an endothermic or an exothermic reaction respectively. The enthalpy change is usually expressed in units of kilojoules per mole, kJ mol^{-1}.

e.g. When 0.20 g of magnesium ribbon is dissolved in 120 cm^3 of dilute hydrochloric acid (an excess), the temperature rose by 8.6 K. Calculate the enthalpy change per mole of magnesium.

Enthalpy change $= -120 \times 4.2 \times 8.6$ J

$= -4334$ J (Note: negative sign as temperature rises.)

Amount of magnesium used $= 0.20/24.3$ mol (A_r of magnesium is 24.3)

$= 8.23 \times 10^{-3}$ mol

Hence enthalpy change per mole of magnesium $\Delta H = -4334/8.23 \times 10^{-3}$ J mol^{-1}

$= -526600$ J mol^{-1}

$= -526.6$ kJ mol^{-1}

Use of an Enthalpy Cycle. The enthalpy cycle should be built up in stages:

(1)   Write down the balanced equation for the reaction involving the enthalpy change you are to calculate.

(2)   Examine the reactants and products. Choose a reagent that will react with both reactants and products to give the same substances as far as possible.

(3)   If this does not enable you to complete the cycle, examine these substances to see what other simple enthalpy changes are needed to complete the cycle. An example will make this clear.

e.g. When solid magnesium carbonate reacts with an excess of hydrochloric acid the enthalpy change is found to be -90 kilojoules per mole of magnesium carbonate. The enthalpy change of formation of $H_2O(l)$ is -285 kJ mol^{-1} and of CO_2 is -393 kJ mol^{-1}. Use these data and the enthalpy change from the example above (for the reaction of magnesium with excess hydrochloric acid) to calculate the enthalpy of formation of $MgCO_3(s)$.

$$(1)$$
$$Mg(s) \;+\; C(s) \;+\; 3/2O_2(g) \;\rightarrow\; MgCO_3(s)$$
$$\downarrow (2) \quad + \quad 2HCl(aq) \qquad\qquad \downarrow (2) + 2HCl(aq)$$
$$(3)$$
$$MgCl_2(aq) + H_2(g) + C(s) + 3/2O_2(g) \rightarrow MgCl_2(aq) + H_2O(l) + CO_2(g)$$

note:

(1)   The equation for the reaction for the enthalpy of formation of magnesium carbonate.

(2)   Both the reactant magnesium and the product magnesium carbonate react with hydrochloric acid to produce magnesium chloride. The appropriate equations are written vertically. Substances which are not involved in these reactions are carried forward (e.g. carbon). Here we need -526.6 kJ on the left and -90 kJ on the right.

(3)   To complete the cycle, carbon must be converted to carbon dioxide and hydrogen to water. Here we need the sum of the enthalpies of formation of water and carbon dioxide, i.e. $(-285) + (-393)$ kJ.

(4)   We now apply Hess's Law:

$$\Delta H_f = (-285) + (-393) + (-526.6) - (-90) = -1114.6 \text{ kJ mol}^{-1}$$

i.e. the enthalpy of formation of magnesium carbonate is -1114.6 kJ mol^{-1}.

SUMMARY: At the end of this topic you should:

(1)   be familiar with simple experimental methods for finding enthalpy changes,

(2)   know how to apply Hess's Law in order to find an enthalpy change which cannot easily be measured directly,

(3)   be able to carry out calculations associated with enthalpy experiments.

LINKS: A knowledge of enthalpy changes can provide an understanding of many reactions: e.g.

heats of decomposition of Group II carbonates (topic 11) and the preference of benzene for substitution rather than addition reactions (topic 17).

6.2 AN ILLUSTRATION OF HESS'S LAW.

HAZARD WARNING: PELLETS OF POTASSIUM HYDROXIDE CAN CAUSE SEVERE BURNS. CLEAR UP ANY SPILT PELLETS AT ONCE.

In this experiment the enthalpy change on neutralising potassium hydroxide with hydrochloric acid will be found. Two different routes will be used. In the first route the potassium hydroxide is dissolved in water and the solution produced neutralised using the acid. The second route involves diluting the acid followed by reaction of the diluted acid with the solid potassium hydroxide. Each route requires the measurement of two temperature changes and hence two enthalpy changes. It is important to start with the same initial amounts of acid and alkali and to finish with the same volume of solution.

ASSESSMENT: You may be assessed on the accuracy of your results (1.7) and on the calculations involved (1.5).

PROCEDURE: ROUTE 1.

Step (a):

$$KOH(s) + H_2O(l) \rightarrow KOH(aq, 4 \text{ mol dm}^{-3})$$

Step (b):

$$KOH(aq, 4 \text{ mol dm}^{-3}) + HCl(aq, 4 \text{ mol dm}^{-3}) \rightarrow KCl(aq, 2 \text{ mol dm}^{-3}) + H_2O(l)$$

(N.B. The mass of potassium hydroxide used below provides the concentration shown.)

(1)   Weigh an empty sample tube with cap. Record its mass in a copy of Table 6 from the Teachers' Guide.

(2)   Now weigh into the tube 5.6 g of potassium hydroxide pellets. Keep the mass of potassium hydroxide to within ± 0.1 g of this value. The pellets are deliquescent, so keep the cap on the sample tube whilst weighing and the lid on the stock bottle. Record the mass of pellets taken. Do not allow the pellets to come into contact with your skin.

(3)   Place 25 cm³ of water in a plastic cup and record its temperature. Use a thermometer which reads to ± 0.2 °C or better. Estimate the temperature to the nearest 0.1 °C. Also measure the temperature of the acid you are using. Record your temperatures in your copy of Table 6 from the Teachers' Guide.

(4)   Measure 25 cm³ of the 4.0 mol dm⁻³ hydrochloric acid with a measuring cylinder.

(5)   Tip the potassium hydroxide pellets into the water [step (a)], stir gently with the thermometer and record the temperature as soon as the pellets have dissolved. Immediately add 25 cm³ of the 4.0 mol dm⁻³ hydrochloric acid [step (b)], stir and record the temperature.

(6)   From your readings note the temperature changes for steps (a) and (b) in Table 6 from the Teachers' Guide. For the step (b) temperature change, you will need the mean of the acid and alkali temperatures as the latter is higher than the former.

ROUTE 2.

Step (c):

$$HCl(aq, 4 \text{ mol dm}^{-3}) + H_2O(l) \rightarrow HCl(aq, 2 \text{ mol dm}^{-3})$$

Step (d):

$$KOH(s) + HCl(aq, 2 \text{ mol dm}^{-3}) \rightarrow KCl(aq, 2 \text{ mol dm}^{-3}) + H_2O(l)$$

(7) Measure 25 cm³ of water into a clean plastic cup and record its temperature in your copy of Table 6 from the Teachers' Guide. Record the temperature of a 25 cm³ portion of the 4.0 mol dm⁻³ hydrochloric acid.

(8) Weigh a second sample of 5.6 g of potassium hydroxide as before. Record your weighings.

(9) Pour the 25 cm³ portion of acid into the water in the plastic cup [step (c)], stir and record the temperature. Immediately add the potassium hydroxide pellets and stir gently to dissolve [step (d)]. Record the temperature again as soon as they have dissolved.

(10) From your readings note the temperature changes for steps (c) and (d). Your acid and water may not be at quite the same initial temperature so you will need their mean initial temperature in step (c).

CALCULATIONS:

(1) Calculate the heat energy change for each of the four steps, (a) to (d). Take care to use the appropriate volume of the solution for each step.

(2) Convert these heat energy changes to kJ mol⁻¹ and find the sum for the each of the two routes. Take care with your plus and minus signs.

(3) Consider quantifiable errors in your weighings, volume measurements and temperature measurements. Which of these will have a significant effect on your final results? Place a range of error on the enthalpy change for each route.

(4) Do the values you have obtained for the two routes agree within the limits of error you have established? Hess's Law states that the two routes should produce the same net enthalpy change.

6.3 THE INDIRECT DETERMINATION OF AN ENTHALPY CHANGE.

In this experiment an enthalpy change which cannot be measured directly will be found. This enthalpy change is ΔH for the reaction:

$$Na_2CO_3(s) + 10H_2O(l) \rightarrow Na_2CO_3.10H_2O(s)$$

This may be determined from the enthalpy change of solution for (a) anhydrous sodium carbonate and (b) hydrated sodium carbonate.

ASSESSMENT: You may be assessed on the accuracy of your results and on their interpretation. Refer to sections 1.5, 1.7 and 6.1.

PROCEDURE:(a) ANHYDROUS SODIUM CARBONATE.

(1) Take the stoppered boiling tube containing anhydrous sodium carbonate and weigh it to the nearest 0.01 g. Use a copy of Table 7 from the Teachers' Guide in which to record your results.

(2) Pour about 100 cm³ of distilled water into a flask and warm it until the temperature of the water is approximately 27 °C. Using a pipette, transfer 50 cm³ of the warm water to a plastic cup and record its temperature using an accurate thermometer.

(3) Empty your weighed sample of sodium carbonate into the 50 cm³ of water stirring the liquid as you do so. Record the highest steady temperature of the solution using your accurate thermometer.

(4) Reweigh the empty stoppered boiling tube and record the value in Table 7 from the Teachers' Guide. Find the mass of anhydrous sodium carbonate added.

(5) If 4.2 J are required to raise the temperature of 1 cm³ of water by 1 °C, calculate the enthalpy change which occurred on dissolving your sample of anhydrous sodium carbonate.

(6) Calculate the enthalpy change when 1 mole of anhydrous sodium carbonate (M_r = 106) is dissolved in water, i.e. ΔH for the reaction

$$Na_2CO_3(s) + aq \rightarrow Na_2CO_3(aq)$$

(b) HYDRATED SODIUM CARBONATE.

(1) Take the stoppered boiling tube containing hydrated sodium carbonate and weigh it to the nearest 0.01 g. Record the value in a copy of Table 7 from the Teachers' Guide.

(2) Pour about 100 cm^3 of distilled water into a flask and warm it until the temperature of the water is approximately 27 °C. Using a burette, transfer 41.2 cm^3 of the warm water to a clean plastic cup and record its temperature using an accurate thermometer.

(3) Empty your sample of hydrated sodium carbonate into the 41.2 cm^3 of water stirring the liquid as you do so. As the hydrated crystals contain 8.8 cm^3 of water of crystallisation, you will have a total volume of water of 50 cm^3. Record the lowest steady temperature of the solution using your accurate thermometer.

(4) Reweigh the empty stoppered boiling tube and record the value in your copy of Table 7. Find the mass of hydrated sodium carbonate used.

(5) If 4.2 J are required to raise the temperature of 1 cm^3 of the sodium carbonate solution by 1 °C, calculate the enthalpy change which occurred in dissolving your sample of hydrated sodium carbonate.

(6) Calculate the enthalpy change when 1 mole of hydrated sodium carbonate (M_r = 286) is dissolved in water, i.e. ΔH for the reaction:

$$Na_2CO_3.10H_2O(s) + aq \rightarrow Na_2CO_3(aq)$$

(7) Using your results from parts (a) and (b) above, draw a Hess cycle and calculate the enthalpy change that occurs when 1 mole of anhydrous sodium carbonate is converted into 1 mole of hydrated sodium carbonate, i.e. ΔH for the reaction

$$Na_2CO_3(s) + 10H_2O(l) \rightarrow Na_2CO_3.10H_2O(s)$$

6.4 THE HEAT OF DECOMPOSITION OF CALCIUM CARBONATE.

In this experiment you will measure the enthalpy change for the thermal decomposition of calcium carbonate, i.e. ΔH for the reaction

$$CaCO_3(s) \rightarrow CaO(s) + CO_2(g)$$

This cannot be found easily by a direct method. However, both calcium carbonate and calcium oxide dissolve readily in dilute hydrochloric acid. By finding the enthalpy changes for these two reactions, the enthalpy change for the thermal decomposition of calcium carbonate may be found using an enthalpy cycle and Hess's Law.

ASSESSMENT: You may be assessed on the accuracy of your results (1.7) and on their interpretation (1.5 and 6.1). A full description of the method for this experiment is not given so you may also be assessed on your planning skills (see section 1.6).

PROCEDURE: Use plastic cups as in experiments 6.2 and 6.3. You will need to devise suitable tables in which to present your results.

(1) First find the enthalpy change when one mole of calcium carbonate is neutralised by an excess of 2.0 mol dm^{-3} hydrochloric acid. Suitable quantities for your experiment are 30 cm^3 of the acid and between 1.25 and 1.50 g of calcium carbonate.

(2) Secondly, find the enthalpy change when one mole of calcium oxide is neutralised by an excess of hydrochloric acid. Suitable quantities for your experiment are 30 cm^3 of the acid and between 0.75 and 1.0 g of calcium oxide.

43

QUESTIONS:

(1) Calculate the enthalpy change per mole of calcium carbonate for the reaction of calcium carbonate with hydrochloric acid.

(2) Calculate the enthalpy change per mole of calcium oxide for the reaction of calcium oxide with hydrochloric acid.

(3) Why is it necessary to use an excess of acid in these reactions?

(4) Write down the equation for the thermal decomposition of calcium carbonate.

(5) Draw an enthalpy cycle which connects the thermal decomposition with the two reactions that you have investigated.

(6) Hence determine the heat of thermal decomposition of calcium carbonate in kJ per mole of calcium carbonate.

6.5 THE HEAT OF FORMATION OF MAGNESIUM OXIDE.

In this experiment the heat of formation of magnesium oxide is to be found by an indirect method i.e. ΔH_f for the reaction

$$Mg(s) + 1/2O_2(g) \rightarrow MgO(s)$$

ASSESSMENT: You will be assessed on your planning skills (1.6). You may also be assessed on the accuracy of your results (1.7) and on their interpretation (1.5 and 6.1).

You are provided with magnesium ribbon, magnesium oxide powder and a supply of 1.0 mol dm^{-3} hydrochloric acid. You also have access to the usual equipment found in a school chemistry laboratory including a balance weighing to $\pm$ 0.01 g and a thermometer reading to $\pm$ 0.2 °C.

You are required to devise and carry out simple experiments to determine the heat of formation of magnesium oxide by an indirect method. You may not, therefore, use a bomb calorimeter.

Describe your method in a manner suitable for another A-level student to follow. Credit will be given for the clarity of your instructions and suitable choice of apparatus, masses of reagents and volumes of solutions. Credit will also be given for a method producing the most accurate result possible and for tables in which to record results.

Using your results show how to calculate the heat of formation of magnesium oxide given that the heat of formation of water is –285 kJ mol^{-1}. You may assume that the specific heat capacity of water is 4.2 J g^{-1} K^{-1}. If you are unable to draw the appropriate enthalpy cycle you may ask your teacher for help but then you will not gain the mark for producing this yourself.

7. EQUILIBRIA

7.1 Introduction to practical work on equilibrium systems.
7.2 The determination of K_c for an ester hydrolysis.
7.3 The solubility product of calcium hydroxide and the common ion effect.
7.4 pH titrations.
7.5 Determination of pK_a for the aqueous aluminium ion.
7.6 Determination of pK_{In} for an indicator.
7.7 Preparation of a buffer solution.

7.1 INTRODUCTION TO PRACTICAL WORK ON EQUILIBRIUM SYSTEMS.

AIMS: This topic shows that the Equilibrium Law has a wide range of applications. It will be used to investigate an organic reaction, the solubility of a sparingly soluble inorganic compound and the dissociation of weak acids. We shall see how to determine the pH of a solution and to set up a buffer solution of known pH.

THEORY: <u>The Equilibrium Law.</u> In general for the reversible reaction at a given temperature

$$aA + bB \rightleftharpoons cC + dD$$

the ratio

$$\frac{[C]^c_{eqm}[D]^d_{eqm}}{[A]^a_{eqm}[B]^b_{eqm}}$$

$= \text{constant} = K_c$, the equilibrium constant.

The symbols [A], etc refer to the concentrations of A, etc at equilibrium (eqm), raised to the power a, etc, which is the number of moles in the stoichiometric equation.

To determine the equilibrium constant for a given reaction, it is necessary to find a method of determining the concentration of one of the reactants or one of the products at equilibrium. The balanced equation for the reaction, together with the amounts of compounds taken at the start of the reaction, may then be used to determine the other concentrations.

If the equilibrium is slow to be established, it may be possible to analyse the mixture using a chemical method (such as a titration). If the equilibrium is rapidly achieved, a physical method (such as measurement of pH) may be more satisfactory. Alternatively it may be possible to stop the reaction by some means, without altering the equilibrium concentrations.

<u>Solubility Product.</u> An equilibrium constant for sparingly soluble ionic compounds, called the solubility product K_{sp}, is written as follows:

for the general change

$$AB_2(s) \rightleftharpoons A^{2+}(aq) + 2B^-(aq)$$

$$K_{sp} = [A^{2+}(aq)]_{eqm}[B^-(aq)]^2_{eqm} \ mol^3 \ dm^{-9}$$

Note that, as the amount of undissolved solid present does not affect the concentration of a saturated solution, the solid AB_2 does not appear in the solubility product expression.

<u>Acid Dissociation Constant and pH.</u> The pH of an aqueous solution is defined as

$$pH = -\log_{10}[H^+(aq)]_{eqm}$$

For a weak acid which dissociates in solution as follows

$$HA(aq) \rightleftharpoons H^+(aq) + A^-(aq)$$

the acid dissociation constant, K_a, is

$$K_a = \frac{[H^+(aq)]_{eqm}[A^-(aq)]_{eqm}}{[HA(aq)]_{eqm}} \text{ mol dm}^{-3}$$

Sometimes it is more convenient to use pK_a which is $-\log_{10}K_a$.

<u>Indicators.</u> These are weak acids which are one colour when undissociated but a different colour when fully dissociated into ions. Their acid dissociation constants may be written as pK_{In} and it may be shown that

$$pK_{In} = pH + \log_{10}\{[HIn]/[In^-]\}$$

where [HIn] and [In$^-$] are the concentrations of the indicator HIn and its ion In$^-$ (formed by loss of a proton from HIn).

<u>Buffer Solutions.</u> These are solutions which may withstand quite large additions of acid or alkali without significant change in pH. A mixture of a conjugate acid and its conjugate base will act as a buffer solution, providing one of the pair is only weakly dissociated into ions in water. A solution containing both ethanoic acid and sodium ethanoate will act as a buffer solution. It may be shown using the dissociation constant expression that (to a reasonable approximation) for a conjugate acid/base pair

$$pH = pK_a + \log_{10}(c_b/c_a)$$

where c_b = concentration of base and c_a = concentration of acid.

SUMMARY: At the end of this topic you should

(1)   have an understanding of methods involved in the determination of equilibrium constants,

(2)   know how to use a pH meter to follow pH changes during a titration,

(3)   have gained an understanding of indicator theory and buffer theory,

(4)   have considerably improved your ability to plan your own physical chemistry experiments.

LINKS: There are some similarities between methods of determining equilibrium constants and methods of following rates of reaction (Topic 9). A study of redox equilibria is made in Topic 8. Use of acid dissociation constants and pK_a values is made when comparing the acidity of organic acids and the basicity of organic bases. A knowledge of the factors affecting the position of equilibrium is needed for industrial processes (such as the Contact and Haber processes).

7.2 THE DETERMINATION OF K_c FOR AN ESTER HYDROLYSIS.

You are required to design a experiment to determine the equilibrium constant for the hydrolysis of the ester ethyl ethanoate. The equation for the reaction is

$$CH_3CO_2C_2H_5 + H_2O \rightleftharpoons CH_3CO_2H + C_2H_5OH$$

At room temperature, the reaction is slow and requires the use of an acid catalyst. You are provided with some ethyl ethanoate, ethanol, glacial ethanoic acid, concentrated sulphuric acid (for use as catalyst) and 0.50 mol dm^{-3} sodium hydroxide (for analysing your equilibrium mixtures). You may use some, or all, of these reagents and whatever apparatus that you think necessary. You must give an indication of quantities to be used. Remember the position of equilibrium can be approached from either side of the reaction equation.

You may use your notes, including your practical notes. Most A-level texts may also be used; your teachers will tell you if there is one they do not wish you to use. You have 30 minutes for the planning part of the exercise.

ASSESSMENT: if this exercise is being assessed, your teacher will wish to see the following in your plan:

(1) a suitable method for the determination of the concentrations of the reactants and products present at equilibrium,

(2) an indication of how you might check that your mixture had reached equilibrium,

(3) a clear, concise account of the procedure that could be followed by another A-level student,

(4) an indication of how the results would be used to find a value for the equilibrium constant for the reaction,

If subsequently you carry out your plan, your teachers will note whether you are capable of modifying it, if necessary, in the light of experience. If you are in need of assistance, they may be able to prompt you with suitable questions. However, you should not seek too much help as this could reduce your final mark.

7.3 THE SOLUBILITY PRODUCT OF CALCIUM HYDROXIDE AND THE COMMON ION EFFECT.

In this exercise, saturated solutions of calcium hydroxide in water and in 0.100 mol dm^{-3} sodium hydroxide are prepared. The hydroxide ion concentration is then determined by titration using standardised aqueous hydrochloric acid. In order to saturate the solutions of calcium hydroxide fully, they should be set up at least 24 hours before they are required.

ASSESSMENT: This exercise involves both volumetric analysis and interpretation of the results obtained. You should refer to the techniques involving manipulation of volumetric apparatus (2.3) and on the interpretation of results of such work (3.2).

Preparation of the Saturated Solutions of Calcium Hydroxide. Work in pairs for this part of the experiment. One of you places 150 cm^3 of distilled water in a conical flask together with a spatula full of calcium hydroxide. The other uses 150 cm^3 of 0.100 mol dm^{-3} sodium hydroxide in place of the distilled water. Again a spatula full of calcium hydroxide is added. Label each flask, stopper and swirl the contents. The two flasks will provide each of you with sufficient to carry out the rest of the exercise individually. Put the flasks in a safe place until the next practical session.

The Analysis of the Saturated Solutions. The procedure is the same for both solutions. Start by working in pairs, and filter the solutions into two clean, dry 250 cm^3 conical flasks. Stopper these and label. Keep the flasks stoppered when you are not taking samples in order to keep carbon dioxide out. Share these two solutions between you for the rest of the practical. You must work individually for the remainder of this practical exercise.

Pipette 10.0 cm^3 of one of the solutions into a clean 100 cm^3 conical flask and titrate against the 0.050 mol dm^{-3} hydrochloric acid provided. Use screened methyl orange as indicator. A very small drop is needed, the colour change is from green (alkali) to violet (acid). At the end point the solution is nearly colourless (pale grey). It is a very sensitive indicator, a fraction of a drop may take you past this grey colour. Repeat the titration as many times as necessary to obtain a consistent result. Record your results in a suitable table.

Repeat this analysis on the second solution, recording your results in a second table. Label each table clearly.

(1) **Interpretation of Results. The Solubility Product of Calcium Hydroxide. (From the results obtained using the solution in distilled water.)**

State clearly the titration value that you intend to use.

(2) Determine the amount of hydrochloric acid used (in moles).

(3) Hence determine the amount of hydroxide ion present in your saturated solution in distilled water.

(4) Calculate the molar concentration of hydroxide ion in this solution.

(5) From (4), calculate the molar concentration of calcium ions in the solution.

(6) Write the expression for the solubility product of calcium hydroxide in terms of the molar concentrations of the ions involved. Use this expression to calculate the solubility product of calcium hydroxide.

(7) **To Investigate the Common Ion Effect. (From the results obtained using the solution in 0.100 mol dm^{-3} sodium hydroxide.)**

Determine the molar concentration of hydroxide ions.

(8) Your answer to part (7) includes the hydroxide ions from the sodium hydroxide. Calculate the molar concentration of hydroxide ions from the calcium hydroxide.

(9) From (8), calculate the molar concentration of calcium ions.

(10) Now determine the solubility product of the calcium hydroxide. Remember that it is the equilibrium concentrations of ions present that you need in your expression.

(11) Explain why the calcium ion concentration is different in the 0.100 mol dm^{-3} sodium hydroxide from that found in the distilled water. This is the Common Ion Effect.

(12) What has been the effect of the sodium hydroxide on the solubility of the calcium hydroxide?

(13) What possible sources of error can you identify?

(14) For those errors that may be quantified, determine the limits of error that you can place on your two values for the solubility product of calcium hydroxide.

7.4 pH TITRATIONS.

You will only have time to perform this experiment on one acid/base pair. Distribute the possible combinations of strong or weak acids and bases round your group. This will enable you to compare the four possible combinations.

ASSESSMENT: It is unlikely that there will be enough equipment for you to carry out your own experiment. If you are working in pairs, your teacher will watch each of you individually to assess your contribution to the manipulation and organisation of the practical work. The experiment needs two runs, so you can divide the tasks fairly between yourselves. After you have obtained your results, your teacher may assess your understanding of them. You may find the guidelines on interpretation of volumetric analysis results useful (3.2).

PROCEDURE: Pipette 25 cm^3 of one of the 0.1 mol dm^{-3} acids provided into a 150 cm^3 beaker. Add 50 cm^3 of distilled water to this using a measuring cylinder. This is needed to ensure that your pH electrode is properly immersed. Place the beaker on a magnetic stirrer. Put a magnetic follower in the solution in the beaker.

Fill a burette with a 0.1 mol dm^{-3} solution of one of the two alkalis provided. Calibrate a pH meter and electrode using a pH 7.00 buffer solution. Place the electrode in your acid solution so that it is just clear of the magnetic follower. Place the burette of alkali over the beaker so that alkali may be added easily.

Switch on the magnetic stirrer, record the value of the pH and add 1 cm^3 of alkali from the burette. Record the steady value of pH and repeat the addition of alkali. Continue adding alkali and recording pH until you have added about 45 cm^3 alkali.

You should now repeat the experiment. This time take more frequent readings over the range where the pH changed rapidly in the trial run.

Using your second set of results, plot a graph of pH (on the vertical axis) against volume of alkali added. For a complete discussion of this practical exercise you will need sketch graphs of the other titrations carried out in your group. When you have these, answer the following questions.

QUESTIONS:

(1) Bearing in mind that you were provided with 0.100 mol dm^{-3} solutions, what volume of alkali should be needed to neutralise the 25 cm^3 aliquot of acid?

(2) Mark this volume of alkali on your graph. What happens to the change in pH at (or close) to this volume?

(3) Compare the four sets of results.

(4) Describe how they differ at the end-points.

(5) Are there any other differences?

(6) Are there any similarities?

(7) Consider the ethanoic acid/sodium hydroxide titration. Determine the pH when the acid is half neutralised. At this point pH = pK_a for ethanoic acid. Can you explain why? Compare your value to the data book value.

7.5 DETERMINATION OF pK_a FOR THE AQUEOUS ALUMINIUM ION.

In aqueous solution the hydrated aluminium ion is found to be weakly acidic (see section 12.3).

$$[Al(H_2O)_6]^{3+}(aq) \rightleftharpoons [Al(H_2O)_5OH]^{2+}(aq) + H^+(aq)$$

In this experiment the pK_a of the ion is determined by measuring its pH against a set of buffer solutions of known pH. These are made by mixing varying volumes of 0.02 mol dm^{-3} methanoic acid and 0.02 mol dm^{-3} sodium methanoate. The pH of such solutions may be calculated using the formula given in the introduction to this topic. As concentration is directly proportional to the volume of solution taken, we may simplify this formula to

$$pH = pK_a + \log_{10}(V_b/V_a),$$

where V_a, V_b are the volumes of acid and conjugate base taken. This may be written as

$$pH = pK_a + \log_{10}V_b - \log_{10}V_a$$

The pK_a of methanoic acid is 3.8.

ASSESSMENT: You may be assessed on your ability to manipulate the apparatus used. As this includes volumetric apparatus, reference to the techniques section on volumetric analysis may be made (2.3). You may also be assessed on the interpretation of your results. This involves calculation of pH of buffer solutions as well as the desired pK_a value. Refer to the guidance in the introduction on calculations (1.5).

PROCEDURE: Make up the mixtures in Table 7 using two burettes to measure the volumes. The liquids should be run into test tubes clearly marked with the pH values of the mixture you are making. Make a copy of Table 7 and calculate the pH values which are not given. Add 10 drops of bromophenol blue to each tube and mix carefully.

Now measure 10.0 cm^3 of the 0.02 mol dm^{-3} aluminium chloride solution provided and add 10

Volume methanoic acid, V_a/cm^3	9	8	7	6	5	4	3	2	1
Volume sodium methanoate, V_b/cm^3	1	2	3	4	5	6	7	8	9
pH		2.8				3.8			4.8

Table 7: Preparation of Standard Buffer Solutions.

drops of the bromophenol blue.

Match your tube carefully against your buffer solutions and estimate its pH. In making the final comparison, you should hold the tubes against the light.

QUESTIONS:

(1) From the pH of the most closely matching tube, calculate the concentration of hydrogen ions in the aqueous aluminium chloride.

(2) What is the concentration of the $[Al(H_2O)_5OH]^{2+}$ ion in the aqueous aluminium chloride?

(3) Assume that, as it is a weak acid, only a few of the $[Al(H_2O)_6]^{3+}$ ions are dissociated. Calculate the value of K_a. Hence calculate pK_a for this ion.

7.6 DETERMINATION OF pK_{In} FOR AN INDICATOR.

In this experiment, the pK_{In} of bromophenol blue is determined.

ASSESSMENT: You may be assessed on your ability to manipulate the apparatus used. As this includes volumetric apparatus, reference to the techniques section on volumetric analysis may be made (2.3). You may also be assessed on the interpretation of your results. This involves calculation of pH of buffer solutions as well as the desired pK_a value. Refer to the guidance in the introduction on calculations (1.5).

PROCEDURE: Arrange eighteen identical test tubes in pairs, one behind the other in a double row, so that when looking through a pair of tubes the colour seen is due to the solutions in both tubes.

The solution HIn(aq) was prepared by adding a few drops of concentrated hydrochloric acid to the indicator, it thus contains the indicator in its undissociated form. The solution In⁻(aq) was prepared by adding a few drops of concentrated aqueous sodium hydroxide to the indicator, it thus contains the indicator in its fully dissociated form. The concentration of the indicator in both solutions is the same.

Using a burette put 10 cm^3 of distilled water into each of the eighteen tubes. Add drops of HIn(aq) and In⁻(aq) as shown in Table 8. Now prepare a buffer solution of known pH. Mix together, using burettes or 5 cm^3 pipettes, 5.0 cm^3 of 0.02 mol dm^{-3} benzoic acid and 5.0 cm^3 of 0.02 mol dm^{-3} sodium benzoate. Add 10 drops of the bromophenol blue solution, this has the same concentration of indicator as solutions HIn(aq) and In⁻(aq).

Decide which pair of the eighteen tubes matches the colour of the buffer tube most closely. In making the final comparison, hold the selected pair against the light with the buffer solution alongside.

The drops of HIn(aq) and In⁻(aq) in the chosen pair gives the ratio of [HIn]/[In⁻].

Test tube no.	1	2	3	4	5	6	7	8	9
drops of HIn(aq)	1	2	3	4	5	6	7	8	9
Tube	10	11	12	13	14	15	16	17	18
drops of In^-(aq)	9	8	7	6	5	4	3	2	1

Table 8: Tubes for determining the ratio of $[HIn]/[In^-]$.

QUESTIONS:

(1)   The pK_a of benzoic acid is 4.2. Calculate the pH of the buffer solution.

(2)   Your answer to question (1) is the pH corresponding to the colour produced in the chosen pair of tubes. From the ratio of drops of HIn(aq) and In^-(aq) in this pair determine the pK_{In} of the indicator using the formula given in the introduction to this topic.

7.7 PREPARATION OF A BUFFER SOLUTION.

You are to devise a practical method for the preparation of a buffer solution having a pH of 5.0. You are provided with the usual apparatus available in your laboratory including an accurate balance and volumetric glassware. You may **not** use a pH meter. The following chemicals are available: **approximately** 0.1 mol dm^{-3} ethanoic acid solution; 0.100 mol dm^{-3} sodium hydroxide; a range of acid/base indicators; solid sodium ethanoate.

You may use your notes, including practical notes, textbooks and data books. The pK_a of ethanoic acid is 4.76 at 298 K.

ASSESSMENT: You should refer to the guidance given in the introduction concerning planning exercises (1.6). You are asked to show clearly

(1)   the calculation(s) on which your method is based,

(2)   practical instructions for making up the buffer solution. These must include such operations as weighings, use of pipettes or burettes, etc.

8. ELECTROCHEMISTRY AND REDOX EQUILIBRIA

8.1 Introduction to redox equilibria and electrochemistry.
8.2 Redox reactions.
8.3 Measuring e.m.f. and the Daniell cell.
8.4 Measuring some cell e.m.f.s.
8.5 Using standard electrode potentials to predict reactions.

8.1 INTRODUCTION TO REDOX EQUILIBRIA AND ELECTROCHEMISTRY.

AIMS: This topic will introduce you to a quantitative scale of oxidising and reducing power. You will learn that the terms oxidising agent and reducing agent are purely relative. It is possible for the same chemical species to act as an oxidising agent and as a reducing agent. You will see that the principles of equilibria apply to redox reactions. The topic shows how you can use standard electrode potentials to make predictions as to whether two compounds will react.

THEORY: The terms oxidising agent and reducing agent may be defined in a number of ways as shown in Table 9.

BASIS OF DEFINITION	OXIDISING AGENT (OXIDANT)	REDUCING AGENT (REDUCTANT)
Combination with oxygen.	Increases number of oxygen atoms present.	Decreases number of oxygen atoms present.
Combination with hydrogen.	Decreases number of hydrogen atoms present.	Increases number of hydrogen atoms present.
Combination with electrons.	Oxidising agents accept electrons.	Reducing agents are electron donors.
Oxidation number.	Decreases for oxidising agent.	Increases for reducing agent.

Table 9: Definitions of Oxidising and Reducing Agents.

One of the difficulties that pupils experience with oxidation and reduction is that an oxidising agent is itself reduced. Similarly a reducing agent becomes oxidised. For example: copper(II) oxide is reduced to copper metal when heated in hydrogen gas.

$$CuO(s) + H_2(g) \rightarrow Cu(s) + H_2O(l)$$

Here the hydrogen is decreasing the number of oxygen atoms present in the copper(II) oxide. It is clearly a reducing agent. However, the hydrogen has gained an oxygen atom so it is itself oxidised! The oxidising agent is the copper(II) oxide.

Remember oxidations must be accompanied by reductions and vice-versa. That is why they are best referred to as redox reactions. Redox reactions may be defined as reactions involving a transfer of electrons from one reagent to another.

In your study of Chemistry prior to A-level you will have met the activity series and possibly the electrochemical series. These series have the merit in allowing a relative order of oxidising and reducing power to be established. For example, if zinc granules are put into aqueous copper sulphate, you could probably predict that copper metal would be displaced according to the equation:

$$Cu^{2+}(aq) + Zn(s) \rightarrow Cu(s) + Zn^{2+}(aq)$$

The two half equations involved in the above reaction are

$$Cu^{2+}(aq) + 2e^- = Cu(s)$$
$$Zn^{2+}(aq) + 2e^- = Zn(s)$$

It is possible, by separating the two half equations into two half cells, to measure a potential difference between the two half cells. This may be done for many pairs of half equations. By choosing a particular half equation as a reference point a scale of electrode potentials is established. By convention, half equations are written with the electrons on the left when using standard electrode potentials. As the oxidising agent is also on the left, the electrons are preceded by a + sign. The **reducing** agent will thus always appear on the **right** of the half equation.

Standard electrode potentials, $E^{\ominus}$, are the potentials of half cells measured under conditions where no current is drawn against a standard hydrogen electrode. Measurements are made under standard conditions (i.e. 298 K, 1 atm pressure and with 1.00 mol dm^{-3} solutions). The standard electrode potential of the hydrogen electrode is defined as 0.00 V. Practically the standard hydrogen electrode (figure 6) is difficult to set up, requires a hydrogen source and poses a serious hazard to safety. There are other, safer and less cumbersome, electrodes which may be used as reference electrodes. The standard electrode potentials of these are accurately known and hence measurements can still be referred to the hydrogen electrode.

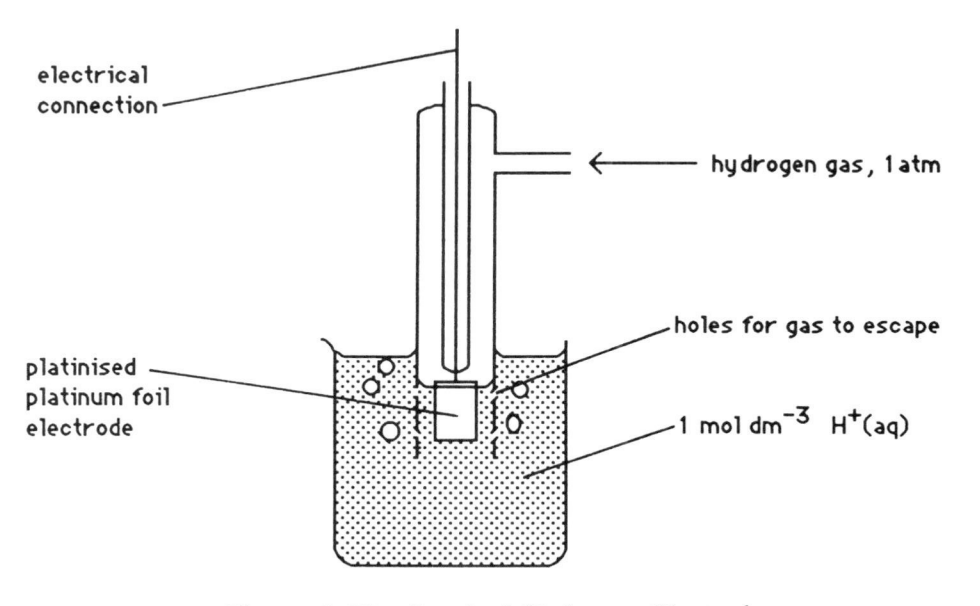

Figure 6: The Standard Hydrogen Electrode

Cell-diagram: This is a diagrammatic way of showing the structure of a cell in chemical terms.

e.g. $Zn(s)|Zn^{2+}(aq):Cu^{2+}(aq)|Cu(s)$ e.m.f. = +1.10 V.

This shows the cell diagram for two half cells joined together, corresponding to the displacement reaction of copper by zinc. The solid vertical lines show a boundary between phases, the colon shows a boundary between two solutions.

Predicting reactions using standard electrode potentials.

e.g. Use standard electrode potentials to decide whether iodide ions will reduce acidified aqueous vanadium(V), VO_2^+.

Look up the $E^\ominus$ values in a data book:

$$E^\ominus / V$$

$$VO_2^+(aq) + 2H^+(aq) + e^- = VO^{2+}(aq) + H_2O(l) \qquad +1.00$$

$$I_2(aq) + e^- = 2I^-(aq) \qquad +0.54$$

Identify oxidising agent: VO_2^+; and reducing agent: $I^-(aq)$. As the reducing agent appears on the right of its half equation, the half reaction moves from right to left, i.e. it is reversed so its electrode potential must be subtracted from that of the oxidising agent.

Hence e.m.f. for the possible reaction $\quad = +1.00 - (+0.54)$ V

$$= +0.46 \text{ V}$$

As this is more positive than +0.3 V, the reaction should occur

$$2VO_2^+(aq) + 4H^+(aq) + 2I^-(aq) \rightarrow 2VO^{2+}(aq) + 2H_2O(l) + I_2(aq)$$

In general if this calculation produces an e.m.f. more positive than about +0.3 V, the reaction should occur. If the e.m.f. is more negative than about –0.3 V, the reaction is not possible. Values of e.m.f. between +0.3 and –0.3 may indicate a reaction under appropriate conditions. If the calculated e.m.f. is 0.00 V, the reactants and products will be in equilibrium under standard conditions, notably with all concentrations at 1.0 mol dm^{-3}.

SUMMARY: At the end of this topic you should:

(1)   have a sound understanding of the terms oxidising agent and reducing agent,

(2)   be able to recognise redox reactions and state which reagents have been oxidised and which reduced,

(3)   appreciate the reversible nature of half reactions,

(4)   know what is meant by the term standard electrode potential,

(5)   know how to measure electrode potentials,

(6)   be able to use standard electrode potentials to make predictions about chemical reactions.

LINKS: this topic extends the principles of equilibria met in Topic 7. Standard electrode potentials are extensively used elsewhere in Topics 13 to 16 inclusive. They will help you to understand and explain the chemistry of many reactions.

8.2 REDOX REACTIONS.

In this practical, you will carry out a number of test tube reactions with the aim of establishing an order of oxidising and reducing power.

PREPARATION FOR THIS PRACTICAL: make a table of definitions of oxidation and reduction. Use the first column of Table 9 as a basis for this. Include an example to illustrate each of the possible definitions.

Using a copy of Table 8 from the Teachers' Guide carry out the reactions given, recording your observations in the spaces provided. Make deductions with the help of the questions provided in the table.

ASSESSMENT: You are reminded of the guidelines on inorganic test tube observation (see 1.2) and deduction (see 1.4) exercises.

You will meet some special tests in this practical for the identification of

- iron(II) in the presence of iron(III) and vice versa;

- distinguishing between an aqueous solution of bromine and one of iodine.

With a few drops of aqueous potassium hexacyanoferrate(III), aqueous iron(II) gives a deep blue precipitate. Aqueous iron(III) gives a green solution with this reagent.

However, aqueous iron(III) will give the same deep blue colour on adding a few drops of aqueous potassium hexacyanoferrate(II). Iron(II) gives a white or pale blue precipitate with this reagent.

In aqueous solution, both iodine and bromine can appear yellow. If the solution is shaken with about 1 cm^3 of 1,1,1-trichloroethane, iodine will colour the organic layer violet, bromine will colour it yellow. 1,1,1-Trichloroethane is denser than water. When you have finished the practical work, answer the following questions:

(1) Place all the half equations in the order that you have established. Draw a vertical arrow on the left to show the order of increasing oxidising power, and a vertical arrow on the right showing increasing reducing power. Remember that your half equations are written:

oxidising agent + electrons = reducing agent

(2) Look up the standard electrode potentials for these half equations. Write these on the left of the equations. What do you notice about the order and signs of these potentials?

(3) Examine the reactions you have carried out in this practical and the standard electrode potentials for the half reactions involved. What do you notice about the potential for the oxidising agent when compared to that of the reducing agent?

8.3 MEASURING E.M.F. AND THE DANIELL CELL.

The e.m.f., or electromotive force, is defined as the potential difference measured under conditions where no current is drawn from a cell. The aim of this experiment is to measure a cell potential whilst drawing a steadily increasing current. Ideally a potentiometer is used to measure a cell e.m.f. However, if only a very small current is drawn from the cell, the potential difference measured differs from the e.m.f. by a millivolt or less.

ASSESSMENT: Your teacher will assess your organisation and manipulation of the electrical equipment (see 1.7).

PROCEDURE:

(1) Set up a Daniell cell as in figure 7.

(2) Connect your cell in series to an ammeter (0–1 A), a rheostat (0–1000 ohm or higher), and a switch. Connect a millivoltmeter/pH meter across the cell. (See figure 7.) Set the meter to read mV.

(3) Set the rheostat to its highest value and close the switch. Note the readings on the millivoltmeter and on the ammeter.

(4) Decrease the resistance from say 1000 to 900 ohm, note the meter readings again.

(5) Continue decreasing the resistance and taking readings. Stop taking readings if the current rises above 0.3 A or when you reach 10 ohm.

(6) What current is flowing when the measured potential difference is at a maximum?

(7) When measuring the maximum potential difference produced by a cell should the resistance be set as high or as low as possible? The resistance of a millivoltmeter/pH meter is such that the potential difference it measures differs from the e.m.f. by 1% or less.

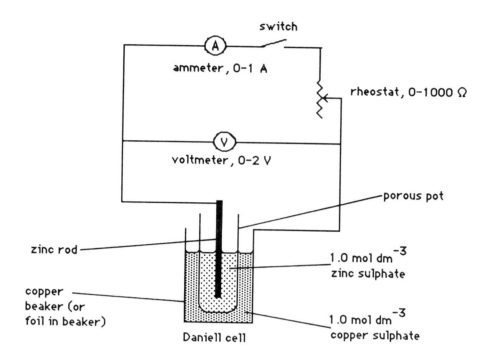

Figure 7: Measuring e.m.f. and the Daniell cell

8.4 MEASURING SOME CELL E.M.F.s.

In this experiment you will set up a number of half cells, connect them together with salt bridges and measure the potential differences they produce.

ASSESSMENT: Your teacher will assess your organisation and manipulation of the electrical equipment (see 1.7). Having made some measurements you will be asked to make some predictions which will also be assessed. Refer to the guidelines on the assessment of interpretations (see 1.4).

PROCEDURE:

(1) Set up a half cell using two 100 cm³ beakers, see figure 8. Bend a strip of copper foil over the rim of one beaker and half fill with 1.00 mol dm⁻³ copper(II) sulphate. Place 1.00 mol dm⁻³ zinc sulphate in the other beaker with a strip of zinc foil bent over the rim. The foils should reach nearly to the bottom of the beakers. The exact size of the foil is unimportant as is the volume of solution. The concentration of the solution does affect the potential difference measured.

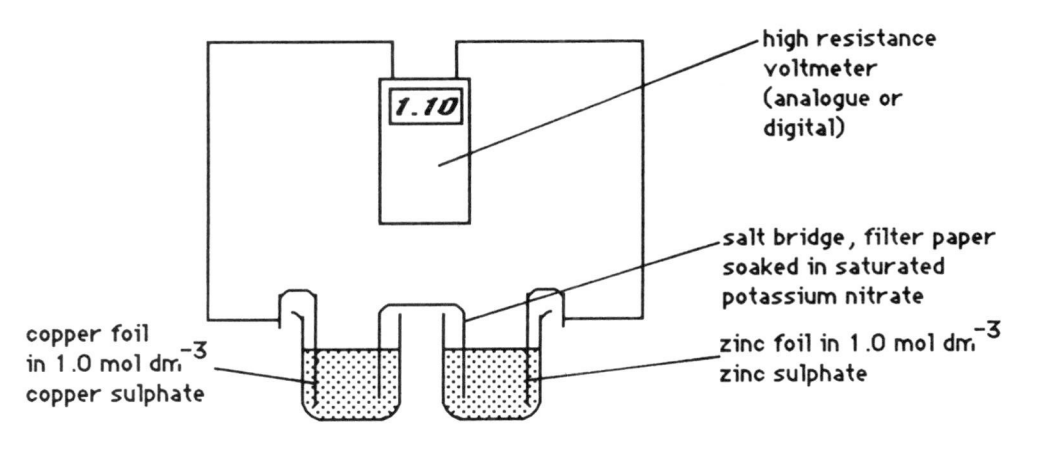

Figure 8: Measuring some cell e.m.f.s.

(2) Set up further half cells as follows. You will not need them all at once, so distribute the work around your group, label the half cells clearly and share them for the measurements.

silver foil in aqueous silver nitrate,
nickel foil in aqueous nickel chloride.

All the solutions are 1.0 mol dm^{-3}, with the exception of the silver nitrate which is 0.025 mol dm^{-3}.

(3) Connect these half cells together in the following pairs by means of salt bridges. Use a filter paper strip soaked in aqueous, saturated potassium nitrate. Measure the potential difference by connecting a mV/pH meter between the foil strips. Use a fresh salt bridge for each pair. Note carefully the polarity of the electrodes. Pairs of half cells:

copper against zinc,
copper against silver,
silver against zinc,
copper against nickel.

(4) Tabulate your results, using the headings shown for Table 10. Notice you need to include the cell diagrams in each case.

Half cell pair	Cell diagram	Potential difference /mV	Positive electrode

Table 10: The Potential Differences of some Cells.

QUESTIONS:

(1) Study the measurements you have made. What do you notice about the value for the silver against zinc half cell when you compare it against the two measurements made using copper?

(2) What values would you predict for the following half cells?

nickel against silver,
nickel against zinc.

Show your predictions to your teacher. Then if you have time you can check them for yourself.

8.5 USING STANDARD ELECTRODE POTENTIALS TO PREDICT REACTIONS.

You will use standard electrode potentials to make some predictions as to whether certain reagents will undergo redox reactions when mixed together. You will then use the predictions to plan suitable test tube experiments to see whether your predictions are confirmed.

ASSESSMENT: Refer to the guidelines in 1.7 on planning exercises. You will be expected to give clear instructions on the tests to be done. You will probably find a tabular presentation best.

PREDICTIONS: Use the table of standard electrode potentials in your data book to decide whether or not the following reagents will undergo reaction. Write balanced equations for the reactions you predict. All the ions are in aqueous solution with concentrations of 1.0 mol dm^{-3}.

(1)   Acidified iron(III) ions with powdered zinc.

(2)   Sulphite ions with acidified manganate(VII) ions.

(3)   Iron(II) ions with silver(I) ions.

(4)   Acidified manganate(VII) ions with granulated tin.

(5)   Acidified vanadyl(V) ions, VO_2^+, with sulphite ions.

Now using your predictions, plan suitable test tube experiments to see whether they are confirmed. You may use the usual reagents found in the laboratory as well as the usual apparatus for such experiments. Another A-level student should be able to follow your plan. Remember to give suitable confirmatory tests for any products.

When you have completed your plan, you may be able to try it out. If you do, some of the solutions will not be 1.0 mol dm^{-3}. In some instances the substances are insufficiently soluble to produce this concentration. Silver nitrate is simply too expensive to use at this concentration. This may affect your predictions but do not worry about changing them.

9. RATES OF REACTION

9.1 Introduction.
9.2 The iodination of propanone.
9.3 The rate of hydrolysis of methyl ethanoate.

9.1 INTRODUCTION.

AIMS: This topic introduces you to some methods for obtaining the rate of a reaction. It also introduces you to the rate equation, rate constant and order of reaction. Finally you should gain an insight into reaction mechanisms and into the nature of catalysis.

THEORY: The rate of a reaction is defined as the rate of change of concentration with time. Hence rate of reaction has units of mol dm^{-3} t^{-1}, where t is in seconds, minutes or even hours. Rates of reaction may be followed by studying the rate of disappearance of a reactant or the rate of appearance of a product.

Chemical reactions usually occur in a sequence of steps. It is this sequence which is called the reaction mechanism. The overall rate of reaction is governed by the slowest of these steps. The rate equation shows how the rate of reaction depends on the concentrations of reagents involved in the slowest step in the mechanism.

For a single step in a reaction,

e.g. $xA + yB \rightarrow C$, where x, y are the moles of A and B respectively needed to produce C.

The rate equation has the form:

Rate of reaction = $k[A]^x[B]^y$, where the constant, k, is known as the rate constant. The powers x and y are known as the orders of reaction for A and B respectively.

At A-level you will normally only meet zero, first or second order reactions (i.e. x and y are 0, 1 or 2). The sum of $x + y$ is known as the overall order of reaction.

The rate constant will have different units for different orders of reaction. For a first order reaction

Rate of reaction = $k[A]$

As rate of reaction has units of mol dm^{-3} $time^{-1}$, k will have units of $time^{-1}$. Work out for yourself the units of the rate constants of a zero order and of a second order reaction.

Design of Experiments: Unless a statistically significant number of results can be obtained, it is important to study the effect of changing one variable at a time. As changes in concentration (and pressure), temperature, particle size and presence of a catalyst all affect reaction rates, careful design of experiments is needed. In order to study the effect of varying concentrations, experiments are often set up in such a way that only one concentration at a time is varied. One way to do this is to set up several different mixtures, with the concentration of just one reagent (or catalyst) being varied. The rate of reaction is then found over the first short period of reaction, during which the rate is effectively constant. The method thus provides a number of initial rates of reaction.

A second method is to follow the change in concentration of a reagent (or catalyst) throughout a reaction. One mixture is used and samples are analysed at time intervals. To enable the effect of one reagent to be studied, all other reagents (and any catalyst) are used in large excess. This means that their concentrations are effectively constant thoughcut the reaction. A graph of concentration against time is plotted and the rates of reaction at different concentrations are found by drawing tangents.

Sometimes it is easier to follow the rate of formation of a product. In this case the reaction is allowed to go to completion. The concentration of a reactant is found as in the following example:

$$\text{for } A + B \rightarrow C$$

If $[C]_t$ is the concentration of product at time t and $[C]_\infty$ is the concentration of product on completion of the reaction,

then $[C]_\infty - [C]_t = [A]_t$

where $[A]_t$ = concentration of reactant A at time t.

These methods enable the order of reaction to be found for individual reagents. Separate study of each reagent (and catalyst, if needed) enables the overall rate equation to be found. The sum of the individual orders will give the overall order and the product of the individual rate constants will give the overall rate constant.

Several methods exist for following changes in concentration. They fall into two categories: (a) A sample is taken and the reaction stopped in some way. This may be done by neutralising an acid reagent or simply by cooling to slow the reaction sufficiently. The mixture is then analysed by, for example, a titrimetric method. This involves destruction of the sample. (b) Concentration is monitored by some change in physical property which may be measured without destruction of all or part of the reaction mixture. For example the change in intensity of the colour of a reagent may be followed using a colorimeter. Changes in pH, conductivity or volume can also provide a means of non-destructively following the rate of a reaction.

SUMMARY: at the end of this topic you should:

(1)   understand what is meant by the terms: rate of reaction, rate equation, order of reaction and rate constant,

(2)   be familiar with some simple methods of studying the rate of reaction,

(3)   know how to obtain the rate equation from the results of such studies,

(4)   understand how the rate equation provides an insight into the reaction mechanism,

(5)   appreciate the effect of catalysts or temperature changes on reaction rates.

LINKS: In Topic 20, the different rates of hydrolysis of organic halogen compounds are studied.

9.2 THE IODINATION OF PROPANONE.

HAZARD WARNING: *MONOIODOPROPANONE IS A LACHRYMATOR.*
RESIDUE DISPOSAL: *POUR YOUR RESIDUES INTO RUNNING WATER*
                          IN A FUME CUPBOARD SINK.

Propanone reacts with iodine solution in the presence of an acid catalyst. The equation for the reaction is

$$CH_3COCH_3 + I_2 \rightarrow CH_3COCH_2I + HI$$

This practical begins with the determination of the order of reaction with respect to iodine. This is done by students individually. If you work in a group of three it is possible to set up different starting concentrations of propanone and of acid catalyst. By comparing the results obtained in your group of three it is possible to obtain the order of reaction with respect to both of these reagents and hence the overall rate equation.

Each student sets up sufficient reaction mixture for samples to be taken for analysis at different times. Analysis is carried out by titration with standard thiosulphate solution to determine the amount of iodine left. The reaction is stopped in the samples by neutralising the acid catalyst present with sodium hydrogencarbonate.

ASSESSMENT: You may be assessed on your manipulative (1.7) or interpretative skills (1.5). You may also find section 2.3 on volumetric techniques useful.

PROCEDURE:

(1) Table 11 shows the different volumes of solution needed for a group of three students. Whichever mixture you take you will be able to determine the order of reaction with respect to iodine. Mixtures 1 and 2 will enable the order with respect to propanone to be found. Mixtures 1 and 3 will enable the order with respect to acid catalyst to be found. Decide who is doing which mixture.

Mixture	1	2	3
propanone/cm^3	5	2.5	2.5
water/cm^3	45	47.5	22.5
1 mol dm^{-3} HCl/cm^3	25	25	50
0.05 mol dm^{-3} I$_2$/cm^3	25	25	25

Table 11: Volumes of Solution Needed for Propanone Iodination.

(2) Measure the volumes of propanone, water and acid required for your mixture into a 250 cm^3 conical flask and mix well. Use burettes for each of these measurements. If there are three of you working together, you can each set up one burette. DO NOT add the iodine at this stage.

(3) Measure 25 cm^3 of the aqueous iodine, using a pipette. Run this into the rest of your reaction mixture. Start your stop clock when about half of the iodine has been added. Mix well again and stopper the flask.

(4) Using a measuring cylinder, place 10 cm^3 portions of 1 mol dm^{-3} sodium hydrogencarbonate into each of five 250 cm^3 conical flasks.

(5) After about five minutes take a 10 cm^3 sample from your reaction mixture, using a pipette. Run the sample into one of the 250 cm^3 conical flasks containing sodium hydrogencarbonate. Note the time when about half of this sample has been run into the sodium hydrogencarbonate.

(6) Take further samples at about 10, 15, 20 and 30 minutes, running each into a fresh portion of sodium hydrogencarbonate.

(7) The contents of each flask are then titrated against the standardised 0.01 mol dm^{-3} sodium thiosulphate provided. Use fresh aqueous starch as an indicator. Record your results in a table showing the time that your samples were taken, all burette readings for the titrations and the volume of sodium thiosulphate required. State clearly in your table heading which mixture you used.

INTERPRETATION OF RESULTS:

(1) Plot a graph of the volume of thiosulphate required (on vertical axis) against the time (on horizontal axis) that each sample was taken.

(2) Write down the balanced equation for the reaction of iodine with thiosulphate ions.

(3) Show how the concentration of iodine in your reaction mixture may be calculated for the first sample only.

(4) In general, how does the concentration of iodine depend on the volume of thiosulphate?

(5) Find the gradient of your graph and convert this to the rate of reaction using your answer to (4).

(6) Does the rate of reaction vary with different concentrations of iodine?

(7) What is the order of reaction with respect to iodine? Write down the rate equation and find the rate constant with respect to iodine.

(8) What are the units of this rate constant?

(9) Obtain the reaction rates for the mixtures investigated by the other two students in your group. What happens to the rate of reaction when the propanone concentration is doubled? Write down the order with respect to propanone. Similarly determine the order with respect to acid catalyst.

(10) Which reagents are involved in the rate determining step of this reaction?

9.3 THE RATE OF HYDROLYSIS OF METHYL ETHANOATE.

Methyl ethanoate hydrolyses more rapidly than ethyl ethanoate at room temperature. It has a more suitable rate for studying in the time available in a lesson. The equation for the reaction is

$$CH_3CO_2CH_3(l) + H_2O(l) \rightarrow CH_3CO_2H(aq) + CH_3OH(aq)$$

The reaction (which is reversible) is catalysed by a strong acid.

In this experiment you will determine the order of reaction with respect to ester concentration and find the rate constant.

ASSESSMENT: You will be assessed on the your plan for the experiment (1.6). This should be presented in a form that could be readily followed by another student.

PROCEDURE:

(1) You are provided with the following chemicals and solutions:

* 5 cm^3 of methyl ethanoate

* 100 cm^3 of 0.5 mol dm^{-3} hydrochloric acid

* standardised 0.200 mol dm^{-3} sodium hydroxide

* ice cold water

* an indicator of your choice.

(2) You have access to the apparatus usually available in a school laboratory.

(3) Devise a method for following the change in concentration of a reactant or of a product using the materials listed in (1) and (2) above. You should note that at temperatures close to 0 °C, the rate of the reaction is very much slower than at room temperature. If the reaction mixture is heated to about 60 °C for about fifteen minutes, the hydrolysis will go to completion.

(4) Use the stoichiometric equation to relate the rate of decrease in ester concentration to the rate of change that you are following.

(5) Show your plan to your teacher before you use it.

(6) Make an appropriate record of your results and use them to find the order of reaction with respect to ester concentration. Also determine the rate constant.

10. PERIODICITY

10.1 Periodicity, an introduction.
10.2 Reactions of the third row elements with oxygen.
10.3 Reactions of the third row elements with chlorine.
10.4 The reactions of the third row oxides.
10.5 The reactions of the third row chlorides.

10.1 PERIODICITY, AN INTRODUCTION.

AIMS: This topic introduces you to the trends and gradations in the chemical reactions of (a) the elements sodium to argon and (b) the oxides and chlorides of these same elements.

THEORY: Before you study the chemical reactions of the third row elements and their compounds, you should study the physical properties of the first twenty elements of the Periodic Table. Whichever physical property is considered (e.g. atomic radius, melting or boiling point, enthalpy of vaporisation, electrical conductivity, first ionisation energy), a repeating pattern of behaviour is found with rising atomic number. Thus the pattern for the second row elements, lithium to neon, is repeated by the third row elements, sodium to argon.

It is this repeating pattern of behaviour which is termed periodicity. It provides the underlying theme on which the Periodic Table is based. Periodicity provides a firm basis on which to build a knowledge and understanding of the elements and their compounds.

Table 12 shows the structures, boiling points and enthalpies of vaporisation for the elements of the second and third rows.

Element	Li	Be	B	C	N	O	F	Ne
Boiling point/K	1615	3243	2823 (sub)	5100	77	90	85	27
Enthalpy of vaporisation /kJ mol^{-1}	134.7	294.6	538.9	716.7	2.8	3.4	3.3	1.8
Structures	←	giant lattices		→	←	molecules →		atoms
Element	Na	Mg	Al	Si	P	S	Cl	Ar
Boiling point/K	1156	1380	2740	2628	553 (white)	718	238	87
Enthalpy of vaporisation /kJ mol^{-1}	89	128.7	293.7	376.8	12.4	9.6	10.2	6.5
Structures	←	giant lattices		→	←	molecules →		atoms

Table 12: Periodicity of Physical Properties.

The elements lithium to carbon have much higher boiling points and enthalpies of vaporisation than the next four elements nitrogen to neon. The two properties also show a steady rise over the first four elements. This pattern is repeated for the elements sodium to argon. The high values are associated with giant lattices, whilst the lower values are associated with simple molecular or atomic structures.

SUMMARY: at the end of these topic you should:

(1) know the observations and equations for the reactions of the elements sodium to argon with oxygen and with chlorine,

(2) understand these reactions in terms of the ability of the elements to act as oxidising and reducing agents,

(3) know how the oxides and chlorides of the elements sodium to argon react with water,

(4) be able to classify the oxides as acids or bases,

(5) know the variation in oxidation number of the elements sodium to chlorine in their simple oxides and chlorides,

(6) be able to use bonding as an aid to the interpretation of these reactions and properties,

(7) understand how atomic and ionic radii, ionisation energies and electronegativities may be used to interpret the observed trends.

LINKS: This topic forms the basis for the next six topics. These deal in detail with elements in groups and blocks as well as with individual elements.

10.2 REACTIONS OF THE THIRD ROW ELEMENTS WITH OXYGEN.

HAZARD WARNINGS: *TAKE CARE WITH THESE REACTIONS, SOME ARE VIGOROUS. KEEP SODIUM WELL AWAY FROM WATER. DO NOT LOOK DIRECTLY AT BURNING MAGNESIUM, THE FLAME PRODUCED IS BRIGHT ENOUGH TO CAUSE EYE DAMAGE.*

RESIDUE DISPOSAL: *DESTROY ANY UNREACTED SODIUM WITH METHYLATED SPIRITS.*

In this practical small samples of the elements sodium to sulphur are burnt in oxygen. Chlorine does not burn in oxygen although several oxides of chlorine are known.

ASSESSMENT: You may be assessed on your manipulative skills (1.7) and/or on your observational skills (1.2). The reactions may be demonstrated to you.

PROCEDURE:

(1) Fill a series of dry gas jars or large test tubes with oxygen from a cylinder. Flush them well with the oxygen, and then cover or stopper them ready for use.

(2) Place a small sample of one of the elements in a combustion spoon. Your sample of sodium should be about 2–3 mm in diameter; remove the oil using dry filter paper and return any unwanted sodium to the stock bottle. Aluminium foil and magnesium ribbon may be held in tongs rather than using a combustion spoon. Use red phosphorus; it is kept under water so heat it gently before the experiment to drive off the water.

(3) Ignite your sample carefully in a bunsen flame and lower the burning sample into one of your gas jars or test tubes of oxygen. Observe what happens. Repeat with the other samples.

(4) At the end of the practical the products of combustion may be shaken with water and the pH of the resulting mixtures found using full range indicator solution. It does not matter if you do not have time to do this as it is investigated further in section 10.4.

(5)   Record your observations in a table.

QUESTIONS:

(1)   Write equations in your table for the reactions which occur. Look up the formulae of the products if necessary.

(2)   As far as possible, place the elements in decreasing order of reactivity with oxygen. They have undergone oxidation, i.e. they are behaving as reducing agents.

(3)   Reducing agents may be defined as reagents that lose electrons. Does the order you have noted in (2) follow the ability of the elements to lose electrons? Justify your answer.

10.3 REACTIONS OF THE THIRD ROW ELEMENTS WITH CHLORINE.

HAZARD WARNING: *CHLORINE MUST BE PREPARED AND USED IN A GOOD FUME CUPBOARD.*

In this practical, small samples of the elements sodium to sulphur are ignited and placed in chlorine gas. A supply of chlorine is obtained by adding concentrated hydrochloric acid to potassium manganate(VII) crystals.

ASSESSMENT: Your teacher will demonstrate the reactions to you. You may be assessed on your observations (see 1.2).

PROCEDURE:

(1)   A small sample of one of the elements is placed in a combustion spoon (or held in tongs as appropriate). The sample is heated gently in a bunsen flame to ignite it. The burning sample is then lowered into a gas jar of chlorine.

(2)   As in experiment 10.2, record your observations in a table.

QUESTIONS:

(1)   Write equations in your table for the reactions which occur. Look up the formulae of the products if necessary.

(2)   Place the elements in order of their reactivity with chlorine. Is this the same order as that obtained for their reactions with oxygen?

(3)   What type of reagent is chlorine in these reactions?

10.4 THE REACTIONS OF THE THIRD ROW OXIDES.

HAZARD WARNINGS: *SODIUM PEROXIDE MAY IGNITE DAMP ORGANIC MATERIAL SUCH AS PAPER.*
PHOSPHORUS(V) OXIDE REACTS VIOLENTLY WITH WATER.
SULPHUR DIOXIDE IS POISONOUS.

You will investigate the solubility in water of the following oxides: sodium oxide, magnesium oxide, aluminium oxide, silicon dioxide, phosphorus(V) oxide and sulphur dioxide. Acidic or basic character may then be found using full range indicator solution. The oxides which prove insoluble in water may be further tested with dilute hydrochloric acid and then with dilute sodium hydroxide to establish their acid/base character.

If sodium oxide is not available use sodium peroxide with care. You may be given sulphur dioxide as an aqueous solution.

ASSESSMENT: Refer to the guidelines on inorganic observational exercises (1.2) and deductive exercises (1.4). You may be assessed on your manipulative skills (1.7) using test tubes (2.2).

PROCEDURE:

(1) Make a copy of Table 13. You will see that it already includes results for chlorine(I) oxide. Allow plenty of space for your observations. (Spread the table over two A4 sheets turned sideways.)

(2) Record the appearance and physical state of each oxide.

(3) Shake a small amount of each solid oxide with about 2 cm^3 of distilled water. Add a few drops of full range indicator solution and note the pH. Find the pH of the sulphur dioxide solution.

(4) For those solid oxides which did not dissolve in water, determine their solubility in (a) dilute hydrochloric acid and (b) dilute sodium hydroxide. Use the solids very sparingly with about 2 cm^3 of the acid or alkali. If they do not dissolve, try warming the mixture.

Name: Date:

Formula of oxide	Na_2O	MgO	Al_2O_3	SiO_2	P_2O_5	SO_2	Cl_2O
Appearance and state.							orange gas
Solubility in water.							soluble
pH of solution							2
Reaction with dilute acid.							——
Reaction with dilute alkali.							——
Classification.							acidic
Structure and bonding.							covalent simple molecule
Formula of highest oxide and oxidation number.							Cl_2O_7 +7

Table 13: Reactions of the Third Row Oxides.

When you have completed the practical work answer the following questions:

(1) Classify your oxides as acids, bases or amphoteric. Record your classification in your table. Describe the trend observed.

(2) Add to your table the structural type (giant lattice or simple molecular) and bonding in each oxide. What generalisation is possible concerning the acid/base character and type of bonding in these oxides?

(3) For the last line of your table write down the formula of the oxide which has the highest oxidation number for each of these elements. Also record the oxidation numbers. What is the trend in these oxidation numbers? Relate the trend in oxidation numbers to the electron configurations of the elements.

10.5 THE REACTIONS OF THE THIRD ROW CHLORIDES.

HAZARD WARNINGS: *MANY OF THE NON-METAL CHLORIDES REACT VIOLENTLY WITH WATER. THEY MUST BE HANDLED IN A FUME CUPBOARD.*

RESIDUE DISPOSAL: *ANY UNUSED CHLORIDE SHOULD BE CAREFULLY DESTROYED BY ADDING SLOWLY TO WATER IN A FUME CUPBOARD.*

The chlorides of the elements sodium to sulphur are each added in turn to water and the pH of the resulting solution found.

ASSESSMENT: In view of the hazards involved in handling some of these chlorides your teacher may demonstrate the reactions to you. If the reactions are demonstrated you may be assessed on your observational record (see 1.2) and the deductions that you make (see 1.4). If you carry out the reactions yourself you may be assessed on your manipulative skills (see 1.7 and 2.2).

PROCEDURE:

(1) Make a copy of Table 14. As with the table for the chemical reactions of the oxides, allow plenty of space for your observations (at least an A4 page turned sideways). Record the appearance and physical state of each chloride.

(2) Look up and record the boiling points of the chlorides using your data book.

(3) Add a small sample of one of the chlorides to about 2 cm^3 of distilled water in a test tube. Determine the pH of the resulting solution using full range indicator. Record your observations in your table. Repeat with each of the other chlorides in turn.

Now answer the following questions:

(1) Write equations for any reactions with water that you have observed.

(2) Describe the trends that you observe in the formulae, volatility and pH of the chloride solutions in water.

(3) Record the structural type (giant lattice or simple molecular) and bonding of the chlorides in your table. Relate the trends that you have found to the structures and bonding of the chlorides.

Name: Date:

Formula of chloride.	NaCl	MgCl$_2$	AlCl$_3$	SiCl$_4$	PCl$_5$	S$_2$Cl$_2$
Appearance and state.						
Boiling point/K.						
Reaction with water.						
pH of solution.						
Structure and bonding.						

Table 14: Reactions of the Third Row Chlorides.

11. S-BLOCK ELEMENTS

11.1 Introduction to s-block elements.
11.2 Flame colours.
11.3 The solubilities of Group II compounds.
11.4 The thermal stabilities of Group II hydroxides, carbonates and nitrates.

11.1 INTRODUCTION TO S-BLOCK ELEMENTS.

AIMS: This topic will introduce you to some of the chemistry of Groups I and II. Apart from the colours Group I elements impart to flames, the experiments only involve compounds of Group II elements. You will see how aspects of equilibria and enthalpy changes can help explain patterns of solubility and thermal stability.

THEORY: The names and symbols of the elements in Group I and II are shown in Table 15. All Group I elements have one electron in their outermost s-orbital; all Group II elements have two electrons in their outermost s-orbital. The two groups are together known as the s-block elements as it is the s-orbital which is being filled.

	Group I		Group II	
	Symbol	Name	Symbol	Name
	Li	Lithium	Be	Beryllium
	Na	Sodium	Mg	Magnesium
	K	Potassium	Ca	Calcium
	Rb	Rubidium	Sr	Strontium
	Cs	Caesium	Ba	Barium
	Fr	Francium	Ra	Radium

Table 15: The s-block elements.

As the last two elements, francium and radium, are radioactive they will not be studied.

SUMMARY: At the end of this topic you should know:

(1) the flame colours of the s-block elements,

(2) the trends in solubility of the Group II hydroxides and sulphates,

(3) the effect on the precipitation of the Group II hydroxides by sodium hydroxide, ammonium hydroxide and ammonium hydroxide with ammonium chloride,

(4) the trends in the thermal stability of the Group II hydroxides, carbonates and nitrates,

(5) how to explain the solubility trends of the sulphates in terms of enthalpies of hydration and lattice energies,

(6) how to explain the precipitation of the hydroxides in terms of the various equilibria involved.

LINKS: Some of the precipitation reactions were met in Topic 4. Enthalpy changes were met in Topic 6 and equilibria and solubility products in Topic 7.

11.2 FLAME COLOURS.

HAZARD WARNING: *CONCENTRATED HYDROCHLORIC ACID IS CORROSIVE AND GIVES OFF IRRITATING FUMES.*

DISPOSAL: *POUR INTO RUNNING WATER IN FUME CUPBOARD SINK.*

Chlorides are used for this practical as they tend to be more volatile than other salts, and hence produce coloured flames more readily. You will examine the atomic emission spectra of the s-block elements using a hand held direct vision spectroscope.

ASSESSMENT: Your manipulative skills, including attention to safety, may be assessed.

PROCEDURE:

(1)   To avoid cross-contamination of the samples, this practical is best organised by setting up a station for each chloride around the laboratory. Having done one flame test, you then move on to the next station.

(2)   To set up a station. Place a small amount of the solid chloride on a watch glass. In a 100 cm³ beaker place about 25 cm³ of concentrated hydrochloric acid and cover with a small watch glass. This beaker is best placed in a sink for safety. A lighted bunsen, a pair of tongs, a direct vision spectroscope and a few pieces of nichrome wire complete the station.

(3)   Thoroughly clean a piece of nichrome wire as follows. Heat the wire strongly to red heat in the bunsen flame, plunge it into the concentrated hydrochloric acid and reheat. Repeat until there is no appreciable flame colour.

(4)   To observe the flame colour, dip the cleaned wire in the acid and then into the solid chloride. Now place the wire with the chloride in the flame.

(5)   To observe the spectrum, point the spectroscope slit at the flame. It is best to work in pairs when using the spectroscope, one person using the spectroscope whilst the other manages the flame test. To see the spectra well the laboratory needs to be as dark as is safely possible. Leave used wires at the station, DO NOT take them to another station.

(6)   Record your flame colours against the name of the element in a suitable table. Try to draw at least one of the spectra for future reference.

11.3 THE SOLUBILITIES OF GROUP II COMPOUNDS.

This experiment is divided into two parts. The first part enables the solubilities of the Group II ions with different anions to be studied by precipitation reactions. The anions used are hydroxide and sulphate. The second part enables the effect of different hydroxide concentrations on the precipitation of the Group II hydroxides to be studied.

ASSESSMENT: You may be assessed on your observational (1.2) or interpretative skills (1.4).

PROCEDURE: Part 1.

(1)   Make a copy of Table 16, using a whole sheet of A4 paper. Leave sufficient space in the table to record the trends observed as well as the solubility products of the compounds formed. Add the solubility products after the practical work, together with the correct units, using your data book.

(2)   All the solutions provided are 0.2 mol dm⁻³. Add the anion solutions dropwise to about 2 cm³ of the cation solution. Continue your addition until you have added an equal volume of the anion solution. Your teacher may suggest that you work in groups of four to save time.

(3)   Indicate the trends in decreasing solubility of the Group II compounds in the table using arrows.

Name: Date:
_____

CATION SOLUTION
_____

ANION SOLUTION	$Mg(NO_3)_2(aq)$	$Ca(NO_3)_2(aq)$	$Sr(NO_3)_2(aq)$	$Ba(NO_3)_2(aq)$
NaOH(aq)				
Trend				
K_{sp}/				
$Na_2SO_4(aq)$				
Trend				
K_{sp}/				

Table 16: Solubilities of Group II Hydroxides and Sulphates.

(4) Use the values of solubility products to explain qualitatively why precipitates form in some cases but not in others.

(5) By considering the trend in lattice energies and hydration energies of the Group II metal ions, determine the trend in the enthalpies of solution of the sulphates. You will need to consider the effect of the changing cation radius on these energies. Use this trend to explain your observed trend for the solubilities of the Group II sulphates.

PROCEDURE: Part 2.

(1) Make a copy of Table 17. As in Part 1, your teacher may suggest that you work in groups of four. Different concentrations of hydroxide ion are obtained by using strong or weak alkali. The sodium hydroxide and ammonia solutions are both 0.2 mol dm^{-3} as are the Group II nitrate solutions. Add the alkali solutions dropwise to the metal ion solutions until there is no further change. Record your observations in the table.

(2) Repeat the tests using ammonia solution but add a small spatula full of solid ammonium chloride first. Shake the mixture to dissolve the ammonium chloride before adding the ammonia.

(3) Qualitatively explain any differences in your observations obtained using sodium hydroxide and aqueous ammonia. (You should consider differences in hydroxide ion concentration and the solubility products.)

(4) Consider the equilibria involved to explain the difference in observations made when using magnesium ions with aqueous ammonia on its own and together with ammonium chloride.

11.4 THE THERMAL STABILITIES OF GROUP II HYDROXIDES, CARBONATES AND NITRATES.

Samples of the compounds are heated in small hard glass tubes to establish the relative ease of thermal decomposition and identify the gases evolved. As in experiment 11.3, your teacher may suggest that you work in groups of four.

Name: _____   Date: _____

	CATION SOLUTION			
ANION SOLUTION	$Mg(NO_3)_2(aq)$	$Ca(NO_3)_2(aq)$	$Sr(NO_3)_2(aq)$	$Ba(NO_3)_2(aq)$
$NaOH(aq)$				
$NH_4OH(aq)$ i.e aqueous ammonia.				
$NH_4Cl(s)$ $+ NH_4OH(aq)$				

Table 17: Hydroxide Ion Concentrations and the Solubility of Group II Hydroxides.

ASSESSMENT: You may be assessed on your observational (1.2) or interpretative skills (1.4).

PROCEDURE:

(1) Prepare a table in which to record your observations and the trends down Group II. You will be heating the carbonates, nitrates and hydroxides of magnesium, calcium, strontium and barium. It is important to use the same rate of heating to obtain the trends.

(2) For the carbonates, the small hard glass tube is fitted with a right angle delivery tube. The carbon dioxide evolved is then passed through lime water. By noting the time taken for this to begin to turn milky, the trend in thermal stability may be found.

(3) Two gases may be identified on heating anhydrous nitrates. As one of these is coloured, the time taken to produce the first hint of colour will give an indication of the trend in thermal stability.

(4) Water is evolved on heating the hydroxides. If the tube is held horizontally, this will condense on the cooler mouth of the tube. Hence an indication of the trend in thermal stability may be found.

(5) Write balanced equations for the reactions observed.

12. ALUMINIUM

12.1 Introduction to aluminium.
12.2 Properties of the element aluminium.
12.3 The properties of the aqueous aluminium ion.

12.1 INTRODUCTION TO ALUMINIUM.

AIMS: In this topic the physical and chemical properties of aluminium and its compounds will be investigated. The aqueous behaviour of the Al^{3+} ion will also be investigated.

THEORY: Aluminium is in the third row of the Periodic Table in Group III. In the third row it lies between the reactive metal magnesium and the non-metal silicon. In Group III, aluminium lies between the non-metal boron and gallium, which is predominantly metallic. Thus we might expect aluminium to show properties typical of both a metal and a non-metal. The acid-base behaviour of its oxide and the structure, bonding and properties of its chloride are good examples of behaviour which is intermediate between that of metals and non-metals.

Much of this intermediate behaviour can be related to the small size and high charge density of the Al^{3+} ion. The ionic radii of the ions of the first three elements in the third row of the Periodic Table are given in Table 18.

Ion	Ionic radius /nm
Na^+	0.102
Mg^{2+}	0.072
Al^{3+}	0.053

Table 18: Ionic Radii.

The aqueous aluminium ion is best written as $[Al(H_2O)_6]^{3+}$. The polar water molecules are strongly attracted to the small positively charged aluminium ion to form a complex ion. Such ions are particularly common amongst the transition elements.

SUMMARY: At the end of this section you should:

(1)   understand why aluminium compounds show both ionic and covalent characteristics,

(2)   know how the corrosion resistance, low density and electrical conductivity of aluminium have contributed to its many successful uses,

(3)   have learnt some of the simple chemistry of aluminium, its compounds and its aqueous ions.

LINKS: The intermediate behaviour of aluminium was first met in the study of the Periodic Table in Topic 10. The transition elements (Topic 16) also show this kind of intermediate, transitional, behaviour. The reactions involving the Al^{3+} ion were first met in Topic 4 (qualitative inorganic analysis).

12.2 PROPERTIES OF THE ELEMENT ALUMINIUM.

ASSESSMENT: You are reminded of the general guidelines on inorganic test tube observations and deductions (see 1.2 and 1.4).

Look up the density, tensile strength, thermal and electrical conductivity of aluminium and of steel in your data book. Record this information in your practical account. You will need a copy of Table 9 from the Teachers' Guide. Carry out test tube reactions, and record your observations and your deductions, using the questions provided.

PROBLEMS:

(1) Can you explain the corrosion resistance of aluminium?

(2) Why is aluminium used extensively for window and door frames?

(3) What properties of aluminium are important in determining its use in (i) aircraft and (ii) saucepans?

(4) Use your data book to compare the relative costs of aluminium, iron and copper in terms of (i) mass and (ii) volume.

The low density and high electrical conductivity (low electrical resistivity) of aluminium enable it to be used in overhead power lines. As its density is much lower than that of copper, the pylons do not have to carry so much weight. Hence they do not need to be so robust, with a consequent saving in cost. However the tensile strength of pure aluminium is too low and the cables are reinforced with a steel core.

(5) With reference to your observations, suggest why aluminium is obtained electrolytically rather than by chemical reduction.

12.3 THE PROPERTIES OF THE AQUEOUS ALUMINIUM ION.

ASSESSMENT: You are reminded of the general guidelines on inorganic test tube reactions involving observation and deduction (see 1.2 and 1.4). You should also consider your results obtained with aluminium oxide in Topic 10. In your equations the aqueous aluminium ion should be represented as $[Al(H_2O)_6]^{3+}$. You will need a copy of Table 10 from the Teachers' Guide.

Carry out the test tube reactions given in Table 10 from the Teachers' Guide, record your observation and deductions in the spaces provided and answer the questions.

13. GROUP IV, CARBON TO LEAD

13.1 Introduction to Group IV.
13.2 The Group IV tetrachlorides.
13.3 The Group IV oxides.
13.4 The solubility of lead(II) compounds.
13.5 Redox properties of the +2 and +4 oxidation numbers.

13.1 INTRODUCTION TO GROUP IV.

AIMS: This topic is intended to illustrate the way in which Group IV elements and their compounds provide a bridge between the metallic and non-metallic elements.

THEORY: The elements of Group IV are shown in Table 19 with their first four ionisation energies and standard electrode potentials for the +2/+4 half reactions.

Element	Symbol	Ionisation Energies/kJ mol^{-1}				Standard Electrode Potential $E^{\ominus}$/V
		1st	2nd	3rd	4th	
Carbon	C	1090	2350	4610	6220	
Silicon	Si	786	1580	3230	4360	
Germanium	Ge	762	1540	3300	4390	
Tin	Sn	707	1410	2940	3930	$Sn^{4+} + 2e^- = Sn^{2+}$ +0.15
Lead	Pb	716	1450	3080	4080	$Pb^{4+} + 2e^- = Pb^{2+}$ +1.69

Table 19: The Elements of Group IV.

In no other group of the Periodic Table is the transition from metallic to non-metallic behaviour demonstrated more clearly than in Group IV. Whilst carbon might well be chosen as a very typical non-metal, the metallic properties of lead and tin have been of service to mankind for thousands of years.

In this topic the trends in behaviour down the group are studied. The change from non-metallic to metallic behaviour is followed by a rise in the energetic stability of the +2 oxidation number at the expense of the +4 number. This produces some important differences in the redox chemistry of tin and lead compounds.

All Group IV elements have a valence shell electron configuration of ns^2np^2. The +2 oxidation number involves the sharing or loss of the two p-electrons whilst the +4 oxidation number usually involves sharing of the four valence electrons in covalent bonds.

SUMMARY: At the end of this topic you should:

(1)   have a sound knowledge of the properties of the Group IV elements and their compounds,

(2)   know the trends in these properties within the group,

(3)   be able to interpret these chemical properties and trends in terms of structure, bonding and (where appropriate) standard electrode potentials.

LINKS: As with the transition elements (Topic 16), the study of Group IV draws together many of the important concepts of A-level Chemistry. Applications of physical chemistry include enthalpy (Topic 6) and standard electrode potentials (Topic 8). Some of the test tube reactions involving lead that you met in Topic 4 are revised.

13.2 THE GROUP IV TETRACHLORIDES.

HAZARD WARNING: *SOME GROUP IV CHLORIDES ARE VERY POISONOUS. SOME ARE ALSO VIOLENTLY REACTIVE, EVEN WITH WATER. CARRY OUT ALL THE REACTIONS IN A FUME CUPBOARD.*

In this practical you will investigate a) the reactions with water and b) the thermal stability of some of the Group IV tetrachlorides.

ASSESSMENT: You may be assessed on your observations (1.2), the interpretation of your results (1.4) or on your planning skills (1.6).

PROCEDURE:

(1) You are provided with small samples ($1 \ cm^3$) of tetrachloromethane, tetrachlorosilane and tin(IV) chloride.

(2) Make a sample of lead (IV) chloride as follows: cool about $5 \ cm^3$ of concentrated hydrochloric acid in a boiling tube standing in a beaker of ice and water. Add a spatula measure of lead(IV) oxide and shake to dissolve the brown oxide. Keep the solution cool until required, it should be clear and yellow. Filter or decant if necessary. This solution contains an equilibrium mixture of lead(IV) chloride and the hexachloroplumbate(IV) ion, $[PbCl_6]^{2-}$.

(3) Decide how you will investigate a) the reactions of these chlorides with water and b) their thermal stability. Write an outline of what you propose to do and show it to your teacher for assessment. Your plan should include reference to, and explanation of, any safety precautions required. You have ten minutes to prepare your plan.

(4) Once your plan has been approved by your teacher, carry out the tests you have devised. Record your observations carefully in an appropriate table.

(5) After the observations have been discussed in class, establish the trends in ease of hydrolysis and thermal stability of these chlorides. What deductions can you make from your observations regarding the nature of any products? Write equations for any reactions seen.

13.3 THE GROUP IV OXIDES.

In this practical you will investigate the acid-base behaviour of some of the Group IV oxides.

ASSESSMENT: You may be assessed on your observations (1.2) or on the interpretation of your results (1.4)

PROCEDURE:

(1) You are provided with $SiO_2(s)$, $SnO(s)$ and $SnO_2(s)$, $PbO(s)$ and $PbO_2(s)$ as well as a source of $CO_2(g)$.

(2) Prepare a table in which you can record the pH of mixtures of these oxides with water, and their behaviour with dilute hydrochloric acid and with aqueous sodium hydroxide.

(3) Mix each of the oxides in turn with distilled water. Determine the pH of the mixture with Universal indicator solution.

(4) Treat small portions of the solid oxides with a few cm^3 of dilute hydrochloric acid. Warm the mixture and note whether the solid dissolves. It is important to use only the smallest

amount of solid if you are to see this clearly.

(5) Repeat part (4) using aqueous sodium hydroxide in place of the acid. Again use the solids very sparingly.

(6) Once the results have been discussed in class, classify the oxides as acidic, basic or amphoteric.

(7) Write balanced equations for any reactions that you have observed.

13.4 THE SOLUBILITY OF LEAD(II) COMPOUNDS.

In this practical you will investigate the solubilty of a number of common lead(II) compounds.

ASSESSMENT: You may be assessed on your observational (1.2) or interpretative (1.4) skills.

PROCEDURE: Carry out the test tube reactions described in Table 11 from the Teachers' Guide, recording your observations in the spaces provided. After you have discussed these in class, record your interpretations of the results in the third column.

13.5 REDOX PROPERTIES OF THE +2 AND +4 OXIDATION NUMBERS.

In this practical you will carry out a number of test tube reactions to investigate the relative stabilities of the +2 and +4 oxidation numbers of tin and lead.

ASSESSMENT: You may be assessed on your observations (1.2) or on their interpretation (1.4).

PROCEDURE:

(1) Carry out the tests described in Table 12 from the Teachers' Guide. In your interpretation you should refer to the standard electrode potentials to be found in your data book. You may wish to carry out further tests to confirm the nature of a product. In such cases describe these extra tests, the observations that you make and their interpretation.

(2) You will need to prepare your own solution of $[PbCl_6]^{2-}$; do this as described in 13.2 for the solution of lead(IV) chloride (part 2 of the procedure for that experiment).

14. NITROGEN AND SULPHUR

14.1 Introduction to sulphur and nitrogen chemistry.
14.2 Redox reactions of sulphur oxyanions.
14.3 Properties of concentrated sulphuric acid.
14.4 Redox reactions of nitrite and nitrate ions.

14.1 INTRODUCTION TO SULPHUR AND NITROGEN CHEMISTRY.

AIMS: This topic will enable you to experience some reactions of nitrogen and sulphur compounds and to gain further experience and confidence in the use of standard electrode potentials in the explanation of redox reactions.

THEORY: Both sulphur and nitrogen show a range of oxidation number in their compounds. The oxidation numbers of compounds and ions with which you should become familiar are shown in Table 20. Table 21 shows the standard electrode potentials for the half reactions that you will need for the compounds of these elements in this topic.

Oxidation Number	Sulphur	Nitrogen
+6	SO_4^{2-} H_2SO_4	
+5		NO_3^- HNO_3
+4	SO_2 SO_3^{2-} H_2SO_3	NO_2
+3		NO_2^- HNO_2
+2	$S_2O_3^{2-}$	NO
+1		
0	S_8	N_2

Table 20: 14.1 Sulphur and Nitrogen Compounds and Ions.

SUMMARY: At the end of this topic you should:

(1) have a sound knowledge of the chemistry of the sulphur and nitrogen oxyanions and of concentrated nitric and sulphuric acids,

(2) where appropriate be able to explain the reactions of these species using standard electrode potentials.

LINKS: Some of these reactions have been met in Topic 4, whilst standard electrode potentials were introduced in Topic 8.

	$E^\ominus$/V
$HNO_2 + H^+ + e^- = NO + H_2O$	+0.99
$NO_3^- + 3H^+ + 2e^- = HNO_2 + H_2O$	+0.94
$NO_3^- + 4H^+ + 3e^- = NO + 2H_2O$	+0.96
$NO_3^- + 2H^+ + e^- = NO_2 + H_2O$	+0.81
$SO_4^{2-} + 4H^+ + 2e^- = H_2SO_3 + H_2O$	+0.17
$S_4O_6^{2-} + 2e^- = 2S_2O_3^{2-}$	+0.09

Table 21: 14.1 Standard Electrode Potentials for Sulphur and Nitrogen Compounds.

14.2 REDOX REACTIONS OF SULPHUR OXYANIONS.

In this practical you will investigate a number of redox reactions involving oxyanions of sulphur and use standard electrode potentials to explain your observations. You will need a copy of Table 13 from the Teachers' Guide.

ASSESSMENT: You may be assessed on your observations (1.2) or on their interpretation after they have been discussed in class (1.4).

PROCEDURE:

(1) Carry out the tests described in Table 13 from the Teachers' Guide, recording your observations in the spaces provided. Remember to identify any gases evolved and to describe the identifying tests.

(2) After completing the experiments and discussing the observations in class, draw conclusions and interpret your results using the standard electrode potentials given in Table 21 above.

(3) Write balanced ionic equations for the reactions observed. You may find the oxidation numbers in Table 20 helpful.

14.3 PROPERTIES OF CONCENTRATED SULPHURIC ACID.

HAZARD WARNING: *CONCENTRATED SULPHURIC ACID IS HIGHLY CORROSIVE.*
DISPOSAL: *POUR SLOWLY INTO COLD RUNNING WATER IN SINK.*

In this practical you will investigate the behaviour of concentrated sulphuric acid as an oxidising agent and as a dehydrating agent. You will find further dehydration reactions of concentrated sulphuric acid in 21.2. You will need a copy of Table 14 from the Teachers' Guide.

ASSESSMENT: You may be assessed on your observations (1.2) or on their interpretation after they have been discussed in class (1.4).

PROCEDURE:

(1) Carry out the tests described in Table 14 from the Teachers' Guide. Remember to identify any gases that you observe and to describe the identifying tests.

(2) After completing the experiments and discussing the observations in class, draw conclusions and, where possible, interpret your results using the standard electrode potentials given in Table 21 above.

(3) Write balanced ionic equations for the reactions observed. You may find the oxidation numbers in Table 20 helpful.

14.4 REDOX REACTIONS OF NITRITE AND NITRATE IONS.

HAZARD WARNING: CONCENTRATED NITRIC ACID IS CORROSIVE.

In this practical you will meet some of the redox reactions involving the nitrite, NO_2^-, and the nitrate, NO_3^-, ions. You will need a copy of Table 15 from the Teachers' Guide.

ASSESSMENT: You may be assessed on your observations (1.2) or on their interpretation after they have been discussed in class (1.4).

PROCEDURE:

(1) Carry out the tests described in Table 15 from the Teachers' Guide. Remember to identify any gases that you observe and to describe the identifying tests.

(2) After completing the experiments and discussing the observations in class, draw conclusions and interpret your results using the standard electrode potentials given in Table 21 above.

(3) Write balanced ionic equations for the reactions observed. You may find the oxidation numbers given in Table 20 helpful.

15. GROUP VII, THE HALOGENS

15.1 Introduction to Group VII.
15.2 The properties of the halogens.
15.3 The preparation and properties of the halogen hydrides.
15.4 Tests for halide ions.

15.1 INTRODUCTION TO GROUP VII.

AIMS: In this topic you will investigate the physical and chemical properties of the halogens, their hydrides and their ions. The understanding you have gained of redox reactions will be used to explain the properties of the elements. This will be an opportunity for you to apply standard electrode potentials.

THEORY: Group VII comprises a group of non-metallic elements on the right hand side of the Periodic Table. As atoms they have an electron configuration with five p-electrons in their highest sub-energy level. Their chemistry is characterised by the completion of this energy level. This can occur in two principal ways:

(1)   the halogen atom gaining one electron to form an ion,

(2)   the halogen atom sharing one or more electrons with other atoms to form a molecule.

In (1) the halogen atom achieves the configuration of the rare gas which has an atomic number which is one more than that of the halogen. The rare gas configuration is also achieved when the halogen atom forms one covalent bond on sharing one of its electrons. However, as indicated in (2), more than one electron may be shared. In this case the number of electrons in the halogen's valency shell normally increases beyond the number in the adjacent rare gas. This can only occur where there are empty d-orbitals with the same principal quantum number as the partially filled halogen p-orbital. Hence this is not possible for fluorine.

A measure of the tendency of the halogens to gain electrons may be seen from their electron affinities (see Table 22). Electron affinity is defined as the energy released when one mole of the gaseous ions forms from one mole of the gaseous atoms. A less well defined measure of the tendency of the atoms to attract electrons is given by their electronegativities. These are also shown in Table 22. Hydrogen has been included for comparison. Fluorine is the most electronegative element, followed by oxygen and nitrogen in that order. Chlorine is the next most electronegative element after nitrogen. The redox behaviour of the halogens may be explained by reference to their standard electrode potentials. These are given in Table 23. Note that these have much more practical relevance than electron affinities or electronegativities. This is because $E^{\ominus}$ values refer to the molecules rather than atoms and to the ions in solution rather than the gaseous ions. You should recall from Topic 8 that the more positive the $E^{\ominus}$ value, the more powerful is the oxidising agent. Hence $F_2(g)$ is an extremely powerful oxidising agent. Similarly, the more negative (less positive) the $E^{\ominus}$ value the more powerful is the reducing agent. Hence, $I^-(aq)$ is a good reducing agent.

SUMMARY: At the end of this topic you should:

(1)   have a sound knowledge of the physical and chemical properties of the halogens, their hydrides and the simple aqueous ions,

(2)   appreciate the trends in these properties in Group VII,

(3)   be able to relate these properties to the position of the halogens in the Periodic Table and to their electron configurations,

(4)   be able to explain their redox reactions using standard electrode potentials.

81

	Electron Affinity /kJ mol^{-1}	Electronegativity (Pauling)
Fluorine	−328.0	4.0
Chlorine	−348.8	3.0
Bromine	−324.6	2.8
Iodine	−295.4	2.5
Hydrogen	− 72.7	2.1

Table 22: The Electron Affinities and Electronegativities of the Halogens.

Half Reaction	Standard Electrode Potential, $E^{\ominus}$/V.
$F_2(g) + 2e^- = 2F^-(aq)$	+2.87
$Cl_2(aq) + 2e^- = 2Cl^-(aq)$	+1.36
$Br_2(aq) + 2e^- = 2Br^-(aq)$	+1.09
$I_2(aq) + 2e^- = 2I^-(aq)$	+0.54

Table 23: The Standard Electrode Potentials of the Halogens.

LINKS: This topic builds upon earlier knowledge gained about chlorine in Topic 10 on the Periodic Table. The electrochemistry introduced in Topic 8 is used to explain the redox reactions of the halogens and their ions.

15.2 THE PROPERTIES OF THE HALOGENS.

In this section we shall examine, by means of test tube reactions, the physical and chemical properties of the Group VII elements chlorine, bromine and iodine. Fluorine is far too dangerous and toxic to be studied in a school laboratory. Indeed it requires very specialised handling techniques.

ASSESSMENT: You are reminded of the guidelines on inorganic test tube observation (1.2) and deduction (1.4).

Before the practical lesson, use your data book to prepare a table showing the physical properties of the halogens, fluorine to iodine inclusive. Record the colour, physical state and boiling point of each halogen in your table. If you have not seen samples of the elements before you will be able to do so during this topic.

The practical work is divided into three subsections, 15.2.1, 15.2.2 and 15.2.3.

15.2.1 SOLUBILITY IN WATER AND 1,1,1-TRICHLOROETHANE.

RESIDUE DISPOSAL: 1,1,1-TRICHLOROETHANE IS IMMISCIBLE WITH WATER.
PLACE RESIDUES IN BEAKER PROVIDED IN FUME CUPBOARD.

Shake aqueous solutions of chlorine, bromine and iodine with 1,1,1-trichloroethane. Make a copy of Table 24 and record your observations in the spaces provided. Does the 1,1,1-trichloroethane form the upper or lower layer? Explain your observations in terms of the intermolecular forces between the halogen molecules and the two solvents.

AQUEOUS HALOGEN SOLUTION	OBSERVATIONS	EXPLANATION
Chlorine		
Bromine		
Iodine		

Table 24: 15.2.1 Investigation of the Solubility of the Halogens.

15.2.2 CHEMICAL PROPERTIES: DISPLACEMENT REACTIONS.

Use a copy of Table 16 from the Teachers' Guide. Carry out the test tube reactions and record your observations in the spaces provided. Shake each mixture with about 1 cm^3 of 1,1,1-trichloroethane to help establish what happens. Record what you deduce the products, if any, of the tests are. Also, in the deductions column, explain your observations using standard electrode potentials. Write a balanced equation for each reaction observed.

15.2.3 CHEMICAL PROPERTIES: REACTION WITH ALKALI.

Add dilute aqueous sodium hydroxide dropwise in turn to the aqueous halogens chlorine, bromine and iodine. Prepare a table for your observations.

After you have completed the practical work, answer the following questions:

(1) With chlorine water and cold, aqueous alkali, a solution of sodium chloride and sodium chlorate(I), NaClO, is formed. Write a balanced equation for the reaction.

(2) Write the oxidation numbers of the chlorine atoms under the equation.

(3) Has the oxidation number of the chlorine changed? Have any other oxidation numbers changed?

(4) What is the oxidising agent? What is the reducing agent?

(5) This type of redox reaction is called a disproportionation reaction. What is the special feature of such a reaction?

(6) A different disproportionation reaction occurs with hot, concentrated sodium hydroxide and chlorine. This time the products are sodium chloride and sodium chlorate(V), $NaClO_3$. Write a balanced equation for this reaction and write the oxidation numbers of the chlorine atoms under the equation.

(7) These reactions of chlorine with sodium hydroxide are of particular industrial and commercial importance. Use your text book to find out what the products are used for. How is the chlorine and sodium hydroxide obtained industrially? Make a note on the process used to obtain these chemicals. Include a labelled diagram and all relevant equations.

(8) Do your observations suggest that bromine and iodine give similar products with cold, dilute sodium hydroxide? Write equations for the reactions possible and name the likely products. List some uses of bromine and iodine and of their compounds.

15.3 THE PREPARATION AND PROPERTIES OF THE HALOGEN HYDRIDES.

HAZARD WARNING: *CONCENTRATED SULPHURIC ACID CORROSIVE.*
    GASES EVOLVED IN THESE REACTIONS ARE TOXIC.

RESIDUE DISPOSAL: *COOL REACTION MIXTURES AND POUR INTO COLD WATER IN FUME CUPBOARD SINK.*

The preparation of the halogen hydrides is investigated using concentrated sulphuric acid (15.3.1) and then concentrated phosphoric acid (15.3.2). The solubility in water and thermal stability of the hydrides of chlorine, bromine and iodine are also investigated in 15.3.2.

15.3.1 PREPARATION OF HALOGEN HYDRIDES USING CONCENTRATED SULPHURIC ACID.

Add about 1 cm^3 of concentrated sulphuric acid dropwise to a small spatula full of solid sodium chloride in a test tube. Cautiously note the appearance of the products and identify the gas(es) evolved. Repeat the test using solid samples of sodium (or potassium) bromide and iodide.

Prepare a table for your results, showing tests carried out to identify gases, your observations and the inferences that you make.

Now answer the following questions:

(1) Is there evidence for the formation of the appropriate halogen hydride, HX (where X is Cl, Br or I), in each test?

(2) Write an equation for the formation of hydrogen chloride from concentrated sulphuric acid and sodium chloride. The other product is sodium hydrogensulphate.

(3) What other type of reaction is occurring where gases other than halogen hydrides are being formed? Write ionic equations for these other reactions.

(4) What can you deduce about the relative ease of oxidation of the halide ions? Does this deduction agree with the standard electrode potentials given in the introduction to this topic? Show any calculations that you make.

(5) Would you choose to use concentrated sulphuric acid for the preparation of any of these halogen hydrides? Justify your answer.

15.3.2 PREPARATION OF HALOGEN HYDRIDES USING PHOSPHORIC ACID.

Add about 1 cm^3 of concentrated phosphoric acid to a spatula full of solid sodium chloride in a test tube. Warm the mixture gently and identify the gas evolved. Collect two test tubes full of the gas as shown in figure 9.

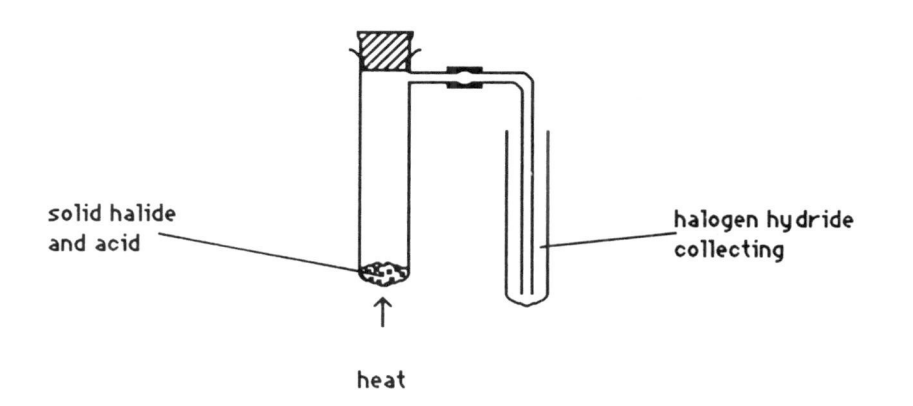

solid halide and acid

halogen hydride collecting

heat

Figure 9: Collection of Halogen Hydrides.

Invert the first tube in a beaker of water and note the solubility of the gas. Heat the end of a glass rod until it glows red then plunge this into the second tube of gas. Look carefully for signs of decomposition. Record all your tests, observations and deductions in a table.

Repeat the tests using solid sodium (or potassium) bromide and iodide.

Write equations for the reactions that you observe in the deductions column of your table. The phosphoric acid produces the dihydrogenphosphate ion, $H_2PO_4^-$, in these reactions. Remember to identify the gases evolved.

When you have completed the practical work, answer the following questions:

(1) Is sulphuric acid or phosphoric acid a better choice for preparing halogen hydrides?

(2) Do these acids produce the halogen hydrides because they are stronger acids or because they are less volatile?

(3) Place the halogen hydrides in order of increasing ease of thermal decomposition. Use your data book to find their enthalpies of formation. Also find the enthalpies of atomisation of hydrogen and the halogens. Use these values to calculate the enthalpy changes for the reactions:

$$HX(g) \rightarrow H(g) + X(g), \text{ where } X = Cl, Br \text{ or } I.$$

Now explain your observed order of thermal decomposition.

(4) Are all the halogen hydrides very soluble in water?

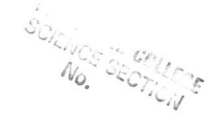

15.4 TESTS FOR HALIDE IONS.

ASSESSMENT: Refer to the guidelines on inorganic observation (1.2) and deduction exercises (1.4).

You are provided with aqueous solutions containing the halide ions fluoride to iodide inclusive. Take each of these solutions in turn and add a few drops of aqueous silver nitrate. Use about 4 cm^3 of each solution. Divide the resulting mixtures into two portions. Place one set of portions in a test tube rack and leave this in the light by the laboratory window for ten minutes.

Take the other set of portions and add an excess of aqueous ammonia to each in turn.

Record your observations on adding silver nitrate, the effect of light and adding aqueous ammonia in a suitable table. Then answer the following questions:

(1) The precipitates that form are the silver halides. What is the trend in solubility of the silver halides?

(2) Write ionic equations for the formation of these silver halides. Include physical states in the equations.

(3) Silver halides decompose in light of the appropriate wavelength. What is the order of photochemical stability in daylight?

(4) The silver halides are decomposed to silver metal by light. Write an equation for the decomposition of silver bromide. What use is made of this reaction?

(5) What is the order of solubility of the silver halides in aqueous ammonia? In aqueous ammonia, the diamminesilver(I) ion, $[Ag(NH_3)_2]^+$ is formed. Write an equation for its formation. It is a linear complex ion; it is also the ion present in Tollen's reagent (see Topic 19). This reagent produces a silver mirror with aldehydes but not with ketones.

16. TRANSITION ELEMENTS

16.1 Introduction.
16.2 Transition element complexes.
    16.2.1 Colours of complexes and oxidation numbers.
    16.2.2 The complex ions of copper(II).
    16.2.3 Colorimetric determination of the formula of a complex ion.
    16.2.4 A complexometric titration.
    16.2.5 Ligands and cobalt stereochemistry.
16.3 Redox reactions.
    16.3.1 Redox reactions involving transition elements.
    16.3.2 Redox reactions of vanadium.
    16.3.3 Ligands and standard electrode potentials.
    16.3.4 Corrosion.
16.4 Catalysis by transition element ions.
16.5 The chemistry of copper(I).
    16.5.1 A comparison of copper(I) oxide with copper(II) oxide.
    16.5.2 The thermal stability of anhydrous copper(II) halides.
    16.5.3 Preparation and properties of copper(I) chloride.

16.1 INTRODUCTION.

AIMS: This topic introduces you to the typical properties of the transition elements. It is a very full topic and your teacher may choose to do only a limited selection of the experiments. The exercises are designed to show you the variety of oxidation states, colours and complex ions of the first row transition elements. You will learn how to find the formulae of complex ions, how ligands affect stereochemistry and standard electrode potentials and you will gain more practice at predicting whether or not redox reactions will occur. An insight into catalytic behaviour will be gained as well as a knowledge of the properties of individual transition elements and their compounds.

THEORY: Transition elements show a variety of characteristic properties including:

* a range of oxidation numbers,

* a much greater range of complexes than other metallic elements,

* coloured compounds,

* catalytic behaviour,

* paramagnetic compounds.

With the exception of paramagnetism, all of these properties are studied in this topic. (Paramagnetism is associated with unpaired electrons.) The study is restricted to elements from the first row of transition elements. These are shown, together with their electron configurations and principal oxidation numbers, in Table 25.

SUMMARY: At the end of this topic you should:

(1) know the colours of the aqueous solutions of the following ions: V^{2+}, V^{3+}, VO^{2+}, VO_2^{2+}, Cr^{3+}, CrO_4^{2-}, $Cr_2O_7^{2-}$, Mn^{2+}, MnO_4^-, Fe^{2+}, Fe^{3+}, Co^{2+}, Ni^{2+}, Cu^{2+},

(2) understand the ligand substitution reactions of copper(II) with water, ammonia and chloride ligands,

(3) be able to determine the formulae of some complex ions using colorimetric and complexometric methods,

Element	Symbol	Electron configuration	Principal oxidation numbers
Scandium	Sc	$[Ar]4s^23d^1$	+3
Titanium	Ti	$[Ar]4s^23d^2$	+4
Vanadium	V	$[Ar]4s^23d^3$	+5, +4, +3, +2
Chromium	Cr	$[Ar]4s^13d^5$	+6, +3
Manganese	Mn	$[Ar]4s^23d^5$	+7, +4, +3, +2
Iron	Fe	$[Ar]4s^23d^6$	+3, +2
Cobalt	Co	$[Ar]4s^23d^7$	+3, +2
Nickel	Ni	$[Ar]4s^23d^8$	+2
Copper	Cu	$[Ar]4s^13d^{10}$	+2, +1

where $[Ar] = 1s^22s^22p^63s^23p^6$, the argon core of electrons.

Table 25: The First Row Transition Elements.

(4) know how different ligands can change the stereochemistry of cobalt(II) complexes,

(5) be familiar with a number of redox reactions involving different transition element ions,

(6) be able to explain these redox reactions using standard electrode potentials,

(7) know how the standard electrode potential for Fe^{3+}/Fe^{2+} is affected by change of ligand,

(8) be able to explain corrosion in electrochemical terms,

(9) understand why the variety of oxidation numbers enables many transition elements to act as catalysts,

(10) be familiar with the chemistry of copper(I).

LINKS: This topic draws together many ideas from all parts of your A-level Chemistry course. You will find many applications of physical chemistry, from enthalpy changes to rates. Many of the experiments involve test tube reactions, some of which you met in Topic 4 (Qualitative Analysis). Tables in that topic will be useful for reference, as will your own tables of tests, observations and conclusions. Topic 3 on Volumetric Analysis and Topic 8 on Redox Equilibria may also be of use.

16.2 TRANSITION ELEMENT COMPLEXES.

16.2.1 COLOURS OF COMPLEXES AND OXIDATION NUMBERS.
In this practical you will meet the colours of some of the different oxidation states of the first row transition elements. You will also meet the colours of some of the simple complex ions.

ASSESSMENT: You may be assessed on your observations (1.2) or on your deductions (1.4). You may also find it helpful to refer to the tests you met in Topic 4.

PROCEDURE:

(1) You will need a copy of Table 17 from the Teachers' Guide. Carry out the tests describ using aqueous solutions of the ions indicated. You are provided with solutions of the ions at their chloride, sulphate or nitrate salts.

(2) Record the colours of these aqueous solutions, and your observations in your copy of Table 17.

(3) What deductions can you make from your observations? Write these in your table together with equations wherever possible. Consult a text book if you are not sure of the reaction products.

16.2.2 THE COMPLEX IONS OF COPPER(II).

In this practical you will investigate the simple complex ions of copper(II) with water, ammonia, edta (ethylenediaminetetraacetic acid) and chloride ions as ligands.

ASSESSMENT: You may be assessed on your observations (see 1.2), your planning skills (see 1.6) and/or your deductions (see 1.4).

PROCEDURE: You are provided with aqueous copper(II) sulphate, concentrated hydrochloric acid, concentrated ammonia and aqueous edta. You also have a supply of test tubes. Carry out tests to find the effect of (a) concentrated hydrochloric acid, (b) concentrated ammonia and (c) aqueous edta on the copper(II) sulphate. Record your observations in tabular form. Having established the colours of the complexes formed with each of these ligands, carry out further tests to establish their relative order of stability. Remember that the aqueous copper sulphate contains complex ions containing water as a ligand.

Look up the stability constants (equilibrium constants) for these ligand exchange reactions in your data book. Use these stability constants to explain the order of stability that you have found. Record your explanations in your table, together with any relevant equations.

16.2.3 COLORIMETRIC DETERMINATION OF THE FORMULA OF A COMPLEX ION.

In this experiment you will find the formula of the complex ion formed between nickel(II) and the hexadentate ligand, ethylenediaminetetraacetic acid (edta). The experiment utilises the change in colour when this complex ion is formed. A colorimeter is used with an appropriate filter to follow the change in absorbance at a narrow band of wavelengths in the visible spectrum.

ASSESSMENT: You may be assessed on your interpretative (1.5) or manipulative skills (1.7).

PROCEDURE:

(1) First, choose an appropriate filter for the colorimeter. Place one of the filters in the colorimeter and half fill a test tube with water. With this tube in the colorimeter, adjust the sensitivity to give a full scale deflection (i.e. zero absorbance). Next mix together equal volumes of the 0.05 mol dm^{-3} nickel(II) chloride and the 0.05 mol dm^{-3} disodium salt of edta in a test tube. Place this tube in the colorimeter and note the meter reading. Repeat the reading using each of the filters in turn. Each time you change the filter you will need to reset the sensitivity of the colorimeter to give a full scale deflection using the tube of water. The best filter is the one that gives the highest reading of absorbance.

(2) Whilst selecting the best filter you may notice that individual test tubes give slightly different readings from each other or when rotated in the colorimeter. For the rest of your experiment you must select a pair which match as closely as possible. Mark this pair clearly so that you always place them in the colorimeter with the correct alignment.

(3) Select nine test tubes and label them 1 to 9. Using burettes, measure the volumes of 0.05 mol dm^{-3} nickel(II) chloride and 0.05 mol dm^{-3} edta shown in Table 26. You will need to copy this table for your results.

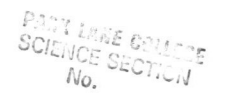

(4) Mix the contents of each tube thoroughly. Using your optically matching tubes, place each mixture in the colorimeter and record its absorbance. Between each reading check that the sensitivity is correctly adjusted for zero absorbance with a tube of water.

Tube Number	1	2	3	4	5	6	7	8	9
Volume Ni^{2+}(aq) /cm^3	9	8	7	6	5	4	3	2	1
Volume edta(aq) /cm^3	1	2	3	4	5	6	7	8	9
Absorbance									

Table 26: 16.2.3 Absorbance Measurements of Nickel(II) edta.

INTERPRETATION OF RESULTS:

(1) Plot a graph of absorbance against the volumes of solution used. As under these conditions absorbance is directly proportional to the concentration of the absorbing substance (Beer's Law), the maximum absorbance on this graph corresponds to the highest concentration of the nickel(II) edta complex ion. This mixture most closely approaches the ratio of nickel(II) to edta in the complex ion.

(2) From your graph, determine the formula of the complex ion.

(3) Draw the full structural formula of this complex ion, clearly showing the charge, the donor atoms and the electron pairs involved in bond formation to the nickel atom.

(4) Finally compare the colour of your solution with that of the filter selected. Using the absorption curves for the filters provided on the colorimeter, explain the difference in colour of your solution and the filter selected.

16.2.4 A COMPLEXOMETRIC TITRATION.

Stability constants of complexes with different ligands vary enormously as do the colours of the complexes. It is possible to choose a potential ligand which forms complexes with high stability constants to titrate aqueous solutions of many metal ions. The disodium salt of edta may be used in this way. In this experiment, iron(III) is titrated against edta. By using solutions of known concentration, it is possible to determine the formula of the iron(III) edta complex ion. To give a clear end point, a little sodium 2-hydroxybenzoate is added to the aqueous iron(III). This gives a blue complex. As the iron(III) edta complex is pale yellow, the end point occurs when the blue solution just turns pale yellow.

ASSESSMENT: You may be assessed on your interpretative (1.5) or manipulative skills (1.7). You may find it useful to refer to section 2.3 and to the work in Topic 3.

PROCEDURE:

(1) Pipette 10 cm^3 of 0.05 mol dm^{-3} iron(III) sulphate into a conical flask.

(2) Add 10 cm^3 of the buffer solution provided (this is 0.8 mol dm^{-3} ethanoic acid and 0.2 mol dm^{-3} sodium ethanoate).

(3) Add about 100 cm^3 of distilled water and 1 cm^3 of 6% solution of sodium 2-hydroxybenzoate.

(4) Titrate against the 0.050 mol dm^{-3} disodium edta until the blue colour just disappears.

(5) Carry out sufficient titrations to obtain a consistent result and tabulate your results.

(6) From your titration value, and the concentrations of the solutions used, determine the formula of the iron(III) edta complex.

(7) Draw the full structural formula of the complex ion.

16.2.5 LIGANDS AND COBALT STEREOCHEMISTRY.

This short practical enables you to study the effect of heat or different ligands on the colours of some cobalt(II) complexes. In these examples the colour changes are associated with changes in the stereochemistry of the complex ions concerned. (Note, many other colour changes with cobalt(II) and other metal ions do not involve changes in stereochemistry.)

ASSESSMENT: You may be assessed on your observational skills (1.2).

PROCEDURE: Carry out the tests given in Table 27. Make a copy of Table 27 in which to record your results.

QUESTIONS:

(1) What do you notice about the effect of the concentrated acid compared to the effect of heat on the cobalt(II) chloride?

(2) The pink colour is due to the octahedral hexaaquocobalt(II) ion. The blue colour is due to the tetrachlorocobalt(II) ion. Draw the structural formula of these ions, showing their shapes and ionic charges clearly.

16.3 REDOX REACTIONS.

16.3.1 REDOX REACTIONS INVOLVING TRANSITION ELEMENTS.

In this practical exercise you are asked to make predictions concerning what might happen on mixing certain reagents. You will need to use a table of standard electrode potentials. Having made predictions, your work may be checked before you go on to carry out the reactions.

ASSESSMENT: This exercise involves a variety of skills some of which might be assessed. These are observational (1.2), deductive (1.4), manipulative (1.7) and planning (1.6) skills. You may find it helpful to refer to tests and observations made in Topic 4.

PROCEDURE:

(1) You will need a copy of Table 18 from the Teachers' Guide. Using standard electrode potentials and the information given, determine the e.m.f. of possible reactions. Note the conditions carefully, particularly with regard to the pH of the mixtures. When your predictions are complete, they may be marked and discussed in class before you proceed with the experiments.

(2) Having made your predictions, carry out the tests on a test tube scale. Wherever possible, identify your products with a suitable test. Be sure to identify any gases evolved.

16.3.2 REDOX REACTIONS OF VANADIUM.

In this practical exercise you are asked to make predictions concerning what might happen on mixing certain reagents. You will need to use a table of standard electrode potentials. Having made predictions, your work may be checked before you go on to carry out the reactions.

ASSESSMENT: This exercise involves a variety of skills some of which might be assessed. These are observational (1.2), deductive (1.4), manipulative (1.7) and planning skills (1.6). You

Name: Date:

TEST	OBSERVATIONS
1. Change of ligand. (a) Add concentrated hydrochloric acid dropwise to about 1 cm^3 of cobalt(II) chloride. (b) To the solution from part (a) above, add water dropwise until there is no further change.	
2. Effect of heat. (a) Warm some pink cobalt(II) chloride paper gently near a bunsen flame. (b) Add a drop of water to the paper from 2(a).	

Table 27: 16.2.5 Ligands and Cobalt Stereochemistry.

may find it helpful to refer to tests and observations made in Topic 4.

PROCEDURE:

(1) You will need a copy of Table 19 from the Teachers' Guide. Using standard electrode potentials and the information given, determine the e.m.f. of possible reactions. The $E^\ominus$ values for the aqueous vanadium ions that you will meet have been included at the top of Table 19. Use your data book for other $E^\ominus$ values. Note the conditions carefully, particularly with regard to the pH of the mixtures. When your predictions are complete, they may be marked and discussed in class before you proceed with the experiments.

(2) Having made your predictions, carry out the tests described on a test tube scale. Wherever possible, be ready to identify your products with a suitable test. Be sure to identify any gases evolved.

16.3.3 LIGANDS AND STANDARD ELECTRODE POTENTIALS.

The standard electrode potentials of metal ions in aqueous solution may change quite considerably if the water ligands are substituted by another ligand. This short practical investigates this for the cobalt(II)/cobalt(III) equilibrium.

ASSESSMENT: You may be assessed on your observational (1.2), deductive (1.4) or manipulative skills (1.7).

PROCEDURE:

(1) Place about 10 cm^3 of aqueous cobalt(II) chloride in a boiling tube. Working in a fume cupboard, add concentrated ammonia dropwise until there is no further change. Note and record the colour change.

(2) Divide the solution into two portions. Keeping one portion as a control, bubble air or oxygen through the second portion until there is no further change. Note the final colour of the solution.

(3) Finally bubble air or oxygen through aqueous cobalt(II).

INTERPRETATION:

(1) Write a balanced equation for the formation of hexaamminecobalt(II) from hexaaquocobalt(II). Underneath the equation write the colours of these complex ions.

(2) Look up the standard electrode potentials for the cobalt(II)/cobalt(III) equilibrium with (a) water as a ligand, (b) ammonia as a ligand and (c) oxygen. Write these down.

(3) Using these standard electrode potentials explain the colour change observed when air or oxygen is drawn through the aqueous hexaamminecobalt(II).

(4) Write a balanced equation for the reaction observed with the air or oxygen.

(5) Why is a similar reaction not observed for the aqueous cobalt(II) ion?

16.3.4 CORROSION.
In this investigation there are three separate experiments. The first of these is the study of the corrosion of two metals in contact. This experiment demonstrates the electrochemical nature of corrosion. The second experiment investigates the corrosion of an iron nail. The third experiment investigates the effect of air (oxygen) on the corrosion of iron.

ASSESSMENT: You may be assessed on your observational skills (1.2) or on your interpretations of your results (1.4).

Experiment 1. Corrosion of Two Metals (Galvanic Corrosion).

(1) Clean strips of copper, zinc and iron using emery paper. The strips should be the same size as a microscope slide.

(2) Wash the strips with propanone on cotton wool to remove grease. Once you have cleaned the strips handle with gloves or tweezers.

(3) Place two strips of different metals in the slots on opposite sides of a microscope slide staining jar.

(4) Place 50 cm^3 of aqueous sodium chloride (0.5 mol dm^{-3}) in the jar and connect the two metal strips with a milliammeter. Record the current flowing (it will not be easy to detect). Make yourself a copy of Table 28 for your results.

(5) Replace the ammeter with a high resistance voltmeter and record the e.m.f. and the signs of the two electrodes.

(6) Repeat for the other couples of metal strips.

(7) Replace the aqueous sodium chloride with distilled water and then with the ferroxyl indicator. Ferroxyl indicator contains potassium hexacyanoferrate(III) and phenolphthalein. Prepare tables similar to Table 28 for your results.

(8) One class set of each metal couple and each solution should be collected together. The metal strips in these should be short circuited using a copper wire and the cells left. Examine them after about one day and then after several days.

Metal couple	Current /mA	Positive electrode	Negative electrode	e.m.f. Observations at electrodes /V positive negative
Fe/Cu				
Cu/Zn				
Zn/Fe				

Table 28: Corrosion of Two Metals in aqueous Sodium Chloride.

QUESTIONS:

(1) Explain the difference in the current measured for the three couples in the distilled water and in the sodium chloride. In your explanation refer to the observations made over a few days in your explanation.

(2) Using your results place the three metals in order of corrosion resistance.

(3) Explain this order in terms of the measured e.m.f.s and in terms of standard electrode potentials. How do your conditions differ from those of the standard electrode potentials?

(4) Make deductions from your observations made over a period of days.

(5) As electrons flow fom the negative electrode to the positive electrode, the latter supplies electrons to the aqueous phase. The positive electrode is thus the cathode of the cell. Similarly the negative electrode is the anode. Refer to Figure 10 and explain your deductions. Write equations to account for any precipitates formed or any colour changes seen.

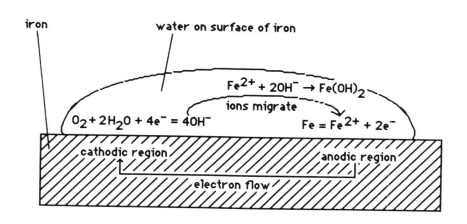

Figure 10: The Electrochemical Explanation of the Corrosion of Iron.

(6) Explain why zinc may be used as a sacrificial anode on the hulls of ships to protect iron from corrosion. Why does copper not offer the same protection?

Experiment 2. The Corrosion of an Iron Nail.

(1) Place a large, clean iron nail in a boiling tube of ferroxyl indicator so that it is half immersed.

(2) Lay a second large, clean iron nail in a Petri dish and cover with ferroxyl indicator.

(3) Leave both nails undisturbed for several days.

(4) Record your observations carefully using diagrams. Label the diagrams clearly to show areas of anodic and cathodic corrosion. Refer to your observations and deductions in experiment 1 above to help you with this labelling.

Experiment 3. The Effect of Differential Aeration on the Corrosion of Iron.

(1) Clean and degrease two strips of iron as in experiment 1.

(2) Place a porous pot in a beaker and fill both the porous pot and the beaker with aqueous sodium chloride. Leave to stand for ten minutes.

(3) Place one iron strip inside the pot with the other outside, in the beaker (see figure 11).

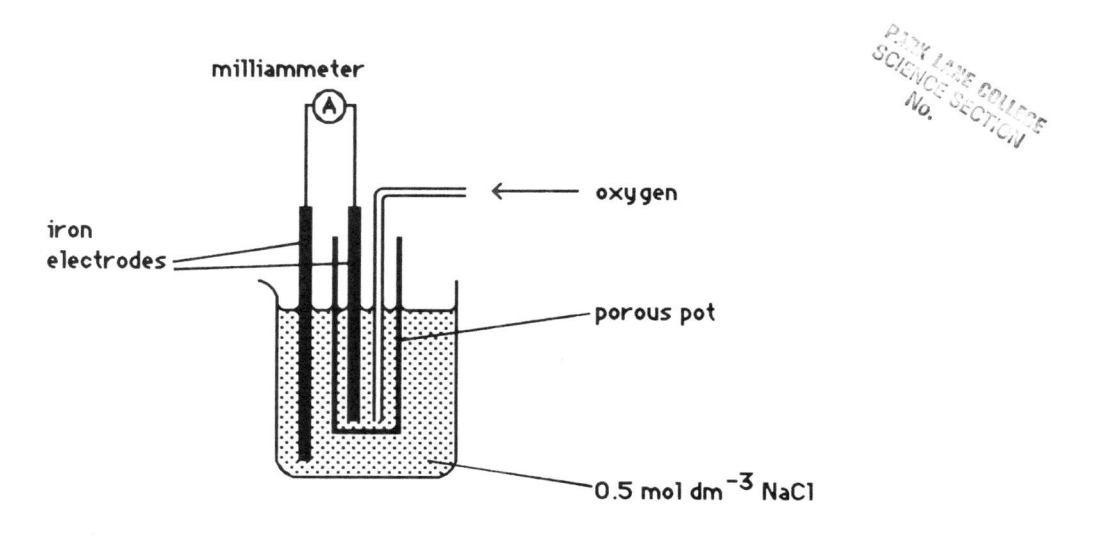

Figure 11: The Effect of Differential Aeration on the Corrosion of Iron.

(4) Connect a milliammeter to the ends of the iron strips. Note the reading.

(5) Bubble oxygen through the aqueous sodium chloride in the porous pot and note the maximum milliammeter reading.

(6) Replace the ammeter with a high resistance voltmeter and renew the aqueous sodium chloride in the porous pot. Note the change in e.m.f. from the time when the oxygen is turned on to the point at which the aqueous phase becomes saturated with oxygen. Note the polarity of the two electrodes.

(7) Select appropriate reagents to identify the products at each of the iron strips. Record the observations that you make with these reagents.

QUESTIONS:

(1) Write equations for the changes occurring at

    (i) the iron strip inside the porous pot,

    (ii) the iron strip outside the porous pot.

(2) Use the results of this experiment to explain why corrosion of a car body takes place from inside the box sections rather than from the outside.

16.4 CATALYSIS BY TRANSITION ELEMENT IONS.

Many transition elements and their ions show catalytic activity. This experiment investigates the effect of iron(II) or iron(III) ions on the reaction of the persulphate ion, $S_2O_8^{2-}$, with iodide ion.

$$S_2O_8^{2-}(aq) + 2I^-(aq) \rightarrow 2SO_4^{2-}(aq) + I_2(aq)$$

The initial rates of the reaction (with or without iron ions) may be compared by incorporating a small volume of aqueous sodium thiosulphate and some starch indicator. The thiosulphate ion will immediately decolorise any iodine formed. Once all the thiosulphate has been used up, iodine will combine with the starch to give the characteristic blue. Thus the time taken for a fixed amount of iodine to form may be found.

ASSESSMENT: You may be assessed on your manipulative skills (1.7) and on the interpretation of your results (1.4).

PROCEDURE:

(1) Using a measuring cylinder, place 10 cm^3 of aqueous potassium iodide and 5 cm^3 of starch indicator in a conical flask. Carefully pipette 10.0 cm^3 of the aqueous sodium thiosulphate provided into this mixture.

(2) Now pipette 25.0 cm^3 of the saturated potassium persulphate solution provided into the conical flask. Mix thoroughly and start timing when you have added about half of the persulphate. Watch the mixture carefullly and stop timing when the blue colour appears.

(3) Repeat the experiment but this time also add 1 cm^3 of aqueous iron(II) sulphate before adding the persulphate.

(4) Repeat the experiment a third time; this time add 1 cm^3 of aqueous iron(III) chloride instead of the iron(II) sulphate.

(5) Collect together the results of others in the class to examine the range of values.

QUESTIONS:

(1) Compare the class results where no aqueous iron has been added. Look particularly at the range of values. Use these values to establish a range of error.

(2) Repeat this comparison for the class results where iron was added.

(3) Considering the experimental range of error found by this method draw a conclusion about the effect of both the iron(II) and the iron(III).

(4) Look up the standard electrode potentials for the two half reactions involving iodine and iron. The value for persulphate is:
$$S_2O_8^{2-} + 2e^- \rightarrow 2SO_4^{2-} \quad E^{\ominus} = + 2.01 \text{ V}$$

Use these values to provide a possible explanation of how either iron(II) or iron(III) might catalyse the reaction of persulphate ion with iodide.

16.5 THE CHEMISTRY OF COPPER(I).

The experiments in this section provide an opportunity for studying an oxidation state of a particular element in more detail. A discussion of this work draws on concepts from many other parts of A-level Chemistry. The section is divided into three subsections.

16.5.1 A COMPARISON OF COPPER(I) OXIDE WITH COPPER(II) OXIDE.

ASSESSMENT: You may be assessed on your observational (1.2), deductive (1.4), or planning skills (1.6).

PROCEDURE:

(1) You are provided with a few grams of copper(I) oxide and of copper(II) oxide. You also have a supply of dilute hydrochloric, nitric and sulphuric acids together with test tubes, a test tube holder and rack and a bunsen burner.

(2) Devise and carry out a simple series of tests to compare the chemical reactions of these two oxides with the dilute acids.

(3) Record your tests, observations and any deductions that you make as clearly as possible.

(4) Write balanced equations for the reactions that you observe.

(5) Use standard electrode potentials to explain why copper(I) salts do not form in aqueous solution.

16.5.2 THE THERMAL STABILITY OF ANHYDROUS COPPER(II) HALIDES.

ASSESSMENT: You may be assessed on your observational (1.2) or deductive skills (1.4).

PROCEDURE:

(1) Heat a sample of anhydrous copper(II) chloride in a small hard glass tube. Identify the gas evolved.

(2) Repeat the experiment using anhydrous copper(II) bromide.

(3) Record your observations and deductions in a suitable manner.

QUESTIONS:

(1) In view of the identity of the gases evolved, what has happened to the oxidation number of copper(II) in these tests?

(2) Write balanced equations for the reactions observed.

(3) Which oxidation number of copper has the greatest thermal stablity? Is this the same oxidation number as that stable in aqueous solutions?

16.5.3 PREPARATION AND PROPERTIES OF COPPER(I) CHLORIDE.

HAZARD WARNING: CONCENTRATED HYDROCHLORIC ACID IS CORROSIVE,
GIVES OFF CHOKING FUMES WHEN HEATED.
USE IN FUME CUPBOARD.

In this practical exercise you will prepare a sample of copper(I) chloride and carry out a few tests on your product. The disproportionation of aqueous copper(I) is easily reversed by first making the dichlorocuprate(I) ion under conditions where it is stabilised. When a solution of this ion is poured into an excess of water, copper(I) chloride is precipitated. The insolubility of copper(I) chloride prevents the disproportionation of copper(I).

ASSESSMENT: You may be assessed on your manipulative skills (1.7).

PROCEDURE:

(1) Working in a fume cupboard, warm about 0.5 g of copper(II) oxide in about 10 cm^3 of concentrated hydrochloric acid.

(2) Now add about 1 g of copper turnings and boil the mixture gently for about 10 minutes.

(3) Now pour the solution into a 250 cm^3 beaker full of distilled water. A white precipitate of copper(I) chloride should form.

(4) Allow the precipitate to settle and then decant off the water.

(5) Place portions of the white solid into three test tubes, it does not matter if a little water is present. Now carry out the following tests using a fresh portion of copper(I) chloride for each test. Record your observations carefully.

  (i) Add aqueous ammonia solution dropwise until the precipitate dissolves. Leave to stand to see if there is any further change.

  (ii) Add concentrated hydrochloric acid dropwise until the precipitate dissolves.

  (iii) Add aqueous sodium thiosulphate dropwise until the precipitate dissolves.

QUESTIONS:

(1) Write an equation for the formation of copper(I) chloride from copper(II) oxide and copper metal.

(2) What is the electron configuration of copper(I)? How does this explain the colour of copper(I) chloride?

(3) Compare the colours obtained on reacting copper(I) chloride or copper(II) ions with aqueous ammonia. Copper(I) forms the colourless diamminecopper(I) complex ion. Copper(II) forms the royal blue tetraamminecopper(II) complex ion. Which other transition element forms a similar colourless ion with ammonia? Write equations for the formation of the copper(I) and copper(II) complex ions with ammonia.

(4) Explain your observations on adding concentrated hydrochloric acid to copper(I) chloride followed by dilution with water. Write balanced equations for the reactions observed.

(5) Thiosulphate and cyanide ions also form complex ions with copper(I) which are stable in aqueous solution. Comment on the effect of these ligands on the disproportionation of copper(I) in aqueous solution.

17. ALKANES, ALKENES and ARENES

17.1 Introduction to hydrocarbons.
17.2 Properties of hexane.
17.3 Properties of cyclohexene.
17.4 Cracking of an alkane.
17.5 Preparation of cyclohexene.
17.6 Properties of arenes.
17.7 Preparation of methyl 3-nitrobenzoate.
17.8 Identification of three unknown hydrocarbons.

17.1 INTRODUCTION TO HYDROCARBONS.

AIMS: The aim of this topic is to investigate the typical physical and chemical properties of the three major groups of hydrocarbons. As all organic compounds contain carbon-carbon single and carbon-hydrogen bonds, it is important to appreciate the properties of molecules which are attributable to these bonds. At a later stage this will enable the properties due to the presence of other functional groups to be identified.

THEORY: There are four major groups of hydrocarbons. These are alkanes, alkenes, alkynes and arenes. With examples these are shown in Table 29. All these compounds contain carbon–hydrogen (C–H) bonds. Arenes are a special group of cyclic hydrocarbons. Other cyclic hydrocarbons include cycloalkanes and cycloalkenes; an example of each of these is given in Table 29.

An understanding of the reactivity of the hydrocarbons is gained by a study of the average bond energies. These are given in Table 30. However, the mechanisms of the reactions are best explained using electron density and bond polarity. All hydrocarbons are essentially non-polar although the electron density in π-bonds is readily polarisable. Our oil based chemical industry relies heavily on alkanes, alkenes and arenes for the manufacture of a very large proportion of organic chemicals. Hence a knowledge of their properties is of fundamental importance. As alkynes are of rather limited value, we shall not study them here.

SUMMARY: At the end of this Topic you should :

(1) Appreciate the added complexity of organic test tube reactions with regard to reaction rate, solubility of reagents, odours and occurrence of side reactions,

(2) Have acquired some skill in synthesis using small scale apparatus (involving reflux, distillation, recrystallisation and use of a separating funnel),

(3) Have met the principles of purifying an organic liquid and an organic solid,

(4) Be able to compare the reactivities of alkanes, alkenes and arenes,

(5) Be able to use suitable reactions to distinguish between different types of hydrocarbon,

(6) Be capable of explaining the properties of hydrocarbons in terms of the bonding present,

(7) Know what is meant by the terms free radical, electrophile and nucleophile.

LINKS: Functional groups may be found attached to all the above types of hydrocarbon skeleton. You must remember that, with certain reagents, reaction may occur with the hydrocarbon part of the molecule as well as with the functional group. Hence you must be thoroughly conversant with the reagents and conditions for the reactions in this topic before going on to other organic topics. You will meet other examples of addition and substitution reactions in later topics.

Hydrocarbon	Name	Structure	Types of Carbon-Carbon Bond
Alkane	Ethane	CH_3CH_3	Single, i.e. σ-bond
Alkene	Ethene	CH_2CH_2	Double, i.e. one σ-bond and one π-bond (localised)
Alkyne	Ethyne	CHCH	Triple, i.e. one σ-bond and two π-bonds (localised)
Arene	Benzene	C_6H_6	six σ-bonds and three π-bonds (delocalised)
Cycloalkane	Cyclo-hexane	C_6H_{12}	σ-bonds
Cycloalkene	Cyclo-hexene	C_6H_{10}	σ-bonds and one π-bond (localised)

Table 29: Types of Hydrocarbon.

Bond	Bond Energy /kJ mol^{-1}
C–H	413
C–C	347
C=C	612
C–C, aromatic	518

Table 30: Bond Energies in Hydrocarbons.

17.2 PROPERTIES OF HEXANE.

HAZARD WARNINGS: *HEXANE INFLAMMABLE.*
CONCENTRATED SULPHURIC ACID CORROSIVE,
REACTS EXOTHERMICALLY WITH WATER.
BROMINE SOLUTIONS CORROSIVE.

RESIDUE DISPOSAL: *PLACE HEXANE RESIDUES IN BEAKER IN FUME CUPBOARD.*
COOL CONCENTRATED SULPHURIC ACID AND POUR SLOWLY
INTO COLD WATER.

ASSESSMENT: You are reminded of the general advice on what your teacher will be looking for in test tube observation and deduction work (see 1.2, 1.3 and 1.4). Ensure that you have carried out the instructions completely and carefully. Advice on techniques using organic reagents in test tube reactions is given in 2.2.5.

Use a copy of Table 20 from the Teachers' Guide for your observations. When you are ready to draw conclusions, use the questions given in the table to help you.

FURTHER STUDY PROBLEMS:

(1) Taking the approximate frequency of visible light as 1×10^{14} s^{-1} and of ultraviolet light as 1×10^{15} s^{-1} calculate the energy available from visible and ultraviolet photons in kJ mol^{-1}. (Use the relationship $E = Lhf$ kJ mol^{-1}, where the Avogadro constant $L = 6.02 \times 10^{23}$ mol^{-1} and Planck's constant $h = 6.62 \times 10^{-37}$ kJ s).

(2) Compare these values to the energy of a bromine–bromine bond. Which photons have enough energy to break the Br–Br bond?

(3) Is the fission of a Br–Br bond likely to be homolytic or heterolytic?

17.3 PROPERTIES OF CYCLOHEXENE.

HAZARD WARNINGS: *CYCLOHEXENE INFLAMMABLE.*
CONCENTRATED SULPHURIC ACID CORROSIVE,
REACTS EXOTHERMICALLY WITH WATER.
BROMINE SOLUTIONS CORROSIVE.

RESIDUE DISPOSAL: *PLACE HEXANE RESIDUES IN BEAKER IN FUME CUPBOARD.*
COOL CONCENTRATED SULPHURIC ACID AND POUR SLOWLY
INTO COLD WATER.

ASSESSMENT: You are reminded of the general advice on what your teacher will be looking for in test tube observation and deduction work (see 1.2, 1.3 and 1.4). Ensure that you have carried out the instructions completely and carefully. Advice on techniques using organic reagents in test tube reactions is given in 2.2.5.

Use a copy of Table 21 from the Teachers' Guide for your observations.

17.4 CRACKING OF AN ALKANE.

The heat energy required to break a typical C–C single bond is high (347 kJ mol^{-1}). However at high temperatures the molecular vibrations in an alkane are sufficiently vigorous for these bonds to be broken. When C–C bonds are broken in alkanes smaller hydrocarbon molecules are formed. The process is known as **cracking**.

In this experiment, a paraffin oil is vaporised and the vapour is passed over heated pumice, which acts as a catalyst. The resulting vapour is cooled and a liquid product collected as well as a gaseous product. Tests are then carried out to determine the types of hydrocarbon present in these two products.

ASSESSMENT: You may be assessed on your manipulative skills (1.7) and/or on your planning skills (1.6).

PROCEDURE:

(1) Set up the apparatus shown in Figure 12. The hard glass boiling tube should contain a large tuft of ceramic or mineral wool soaked in about 3 cm^3 of paraffin oil. Clamp the tube gently at the neck in a horizontal position before placing the pumice inside it.

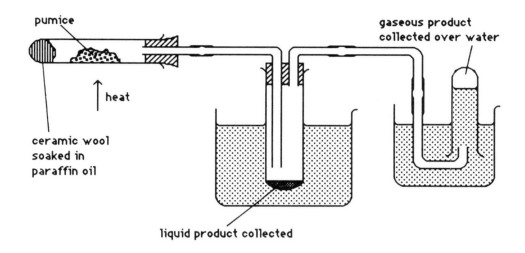

Figure 12: Cracking of an Alkane.

(2) Have several test tubes filled with water ready to collect the gaseous product before you start heating. You will also need some corks to stopper these once you have collected the gas.

(3) Heat the pumice gently at first and then more strongly with a bunsen flame.

(4) When the pumice is hot, occasionally play the flame on the ceramic wool soaked in paraffin oil so as to provide a steady stream of vapour over the hot pumice. Keep heating the pumice.

(5) When you have collected three or four tubes of the gaseous product, stop heating, turn off the bunsen and **at once** remove the bung from the hard glass boiling tube. You should find that you have a little liquid product as well.

(6) Using your knowledge of the reactions and physical properties of alkanes and alkenes, deduce what you can about the nature of the two products. More paraffin oil is available if you wish to use this for comparison. Make a record of any observations that you make and of any tests that you carry out. Record all your deductions clearly.

Now answer the following questions:

(1) Do you have any evidence that the liquid product contains smaller molecules than those in the paraffin oil?

(2) Write an equation (using graphic display formulae) which would give a possible explanation of your observations.

(3) What is the effect of the catalyst on the temperature required for the cracking reaction?

(4) What name would you give to that part of the apparatus in which you collected the liquid product?

(5) The cracking of oil is a very important source of two types of chemical. Suggest two products in everyday use one from each of these two types of chemical.

17.5 PREPARATION OF CYCLOHEXENE.

This preparation makes use of a dehydration reaction of an alcohol, cyclohexanol (see Topic 18).

$$C_6H_{11}OH \rightarrow C_6H_{10} + H_2O$$

i.e. $C_6H_{11}OH \rightarrow C_6H_{10} + H_2O$

Concentrated phosphoric acid is used as the dehydrating agent. The reaction is slow and, in order that the reactant or product are not lost during the period of heating, the technique of **refluxing** is used. The purification of the liquid product will introduce you to the procedure for purifying organic liquids in general. By the end of the experiment you will have gained some expertise in the handling of small scale glass apparatus with interchangeable ground glass joints. You should also have gained some satisfaction in the preparation of a pure sample of the product of a chemical change. Industrially, cyclohexanol is obtained from phenol, which is in turn obtained from benzene via the cumene synthesis.

ASSESSMENT: You are reminded of the general guidance given in the introduction on manipulative skills (see 1.7) and on the use of glassware with interchangeable joints (2.4). After the experiment you should hand in your product, together with your report on the experiment. Note that this should include answers to the questions below and your yield (with calculation) and boiling point of product.

PROCEDURE: 5 cm³ of 85% phosphoric acid are added, a little at a time, to 10 cm³ of cyclohexanol in a 50 cm³ pear shaped flask. Mix well and keep the mixture cooled during the addition using water. Now fit the flask with a condenser for reflux (figure 13). **Note** that the water flows in the same direction as the vapour (parallel flow) to produce the most rapid cooling. A tripod and gauze should now be placed under the flask. Add a boiling chip to the contents of the flask and heat gently with a small flame until the mixture boils. Continue heating for ten minutes, note the ring of condensing vapour at the lower end of the condenser. At the end of this time allow the contents of the flask to cool. Rearrange the condenser, with a still head, thermometer and receiver bend for distillation (figure 14). Heat the mixture gently and collect the fraction which distils over below 90 °C in a small conical flask. **Note** that this time the water flows in the opposite direction to the vapour flow (countercurrent flow). This produces the biggest decrease in temperature for the condensate.

PURIFICATION OF CRUDE PRODUCT: In your report on this experiment answer the questions that follow:

(1) Name some of the impurities present in the crude sample.

(2) You will wash your product with water. Which impurity/ies will the water remove?

(3) After washing with water, which layer should you keep in the separating funnel? Refer back to Experiment 17.4 for information on the density of your product.

(4) What is the purpose of adding anhydrous calcium chloride to your sample after washing your sample with water?

Transfer your crude product to a separating funnel and add an equal volume of water. Stopper and shake the funnel, releasing any build up of pressure by holding the funnel upside down and opening the tap. Any liquid lost through the tap will drain back into the funnel. Be sure to hold the stopper firmly in place whilst doing this! Drain off the lower layer into a clean container. Having decided which layer is the cyclohexene (see question (3)), transfer it to a small conical flask and add a spatula measure of anhydrous calcium chloride. Stopper the flask and swirl the

103

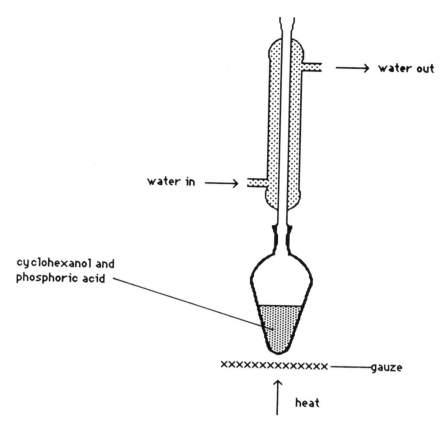

Figure 13: Reflux Apparatus.

contents. If the contents do not become clear after five or ten minutes, or if the calcium chloride dissolves, add more calcium chloride. If it continues to dissolve you have probably got the wrong layer from your separating funnel!

Now filter the liquid through a small plug of glass wool into a clean, dry 50 cm³ pear shaped flask. Set up a clean, dry apparatus for distillation and collect the product which distils between 81 °C and 85 °C in a weighed sample tube.

Weigh your product. Look up the density of cyclohexanol, calculate the mass of cyclohexanol used, and hence the maximum yield of cyclohexene. Express your yield as a percentage of this, theoretical, yield. Label your sample tube with your name, the product name, its boiling range and your percentage yield. How might you test a few drops of your pure product to show that it is an alkene? If you have time you should carry out your suggested test before you hand in your product. Record the observations and deductions that you make when you carry out this test. Your teacher will expect both your sample tube of product and your written report.

17.6 PROPERTIES OF ARENES

As benzene is toxic, methylbenzene is used to study these properties (17.6.1). Although it is much less harmful than benzene, you should still treat it with caution. In order to appreciate fully the reactions of the benzene ring, methoxybenzene is used to study the further reactions of arenes (17.6.2). The presence of the methoxy, CH_3O- group enhances the reactivity of the ring considerably in comparison to the methyl group in methylbenzene.

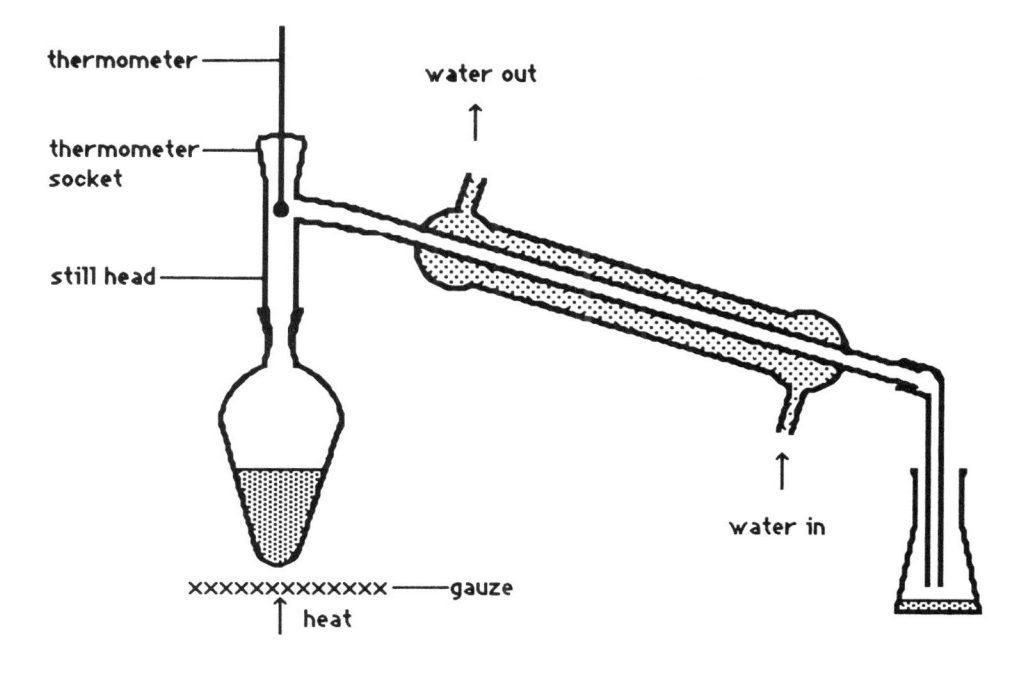

Figure 14: Distillation.

The structures of these arenes are:

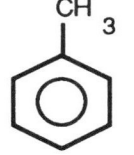

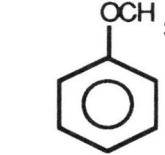

methylbenzene   methoxybenzene

ASSESSMENT: You are reminded of the general advice on what your teacher will be looking for in organic test tube observation and deduction work (see 1.2, 1.3 and 1.4). Ensure that you have carried out the instructions completely and carefully. Advice on techniques using organic reagents in test tube reactions is given in 2.2.5. You should note, when considering your observations, that methylbenzene contains a methyl, CH_3- , group. This may show typical alkane properties.

This practical comes in two parts, 17.6.1 and 17.6.2.

17.6.1 PROPERTIES OF METHYLBENZENE
HAZARD WARNINGS: *METHYLBENZENE INFLAMMABLE.*
                                     CONCENTRATED SULPHURIC ACID CORROSIVE,
                                     REACTS EXOTHERMICALLY WITH WATER.
                                     BROMINE SOLUTIONS CORROSIVE.

RESIDUE DISPOSAL: *PLACE METHYLBENZENE RESIDUES IN BEAKER*
                                     IN FUME CUPBOARD.
                                     COOL CONCENTRATED SULPHURIC ACID AND POUR SLOWLY
                                     INTO COLD WATER.

This part involves the same test reagents and conditions used with hexane and cyclohexene. Use a copy of Table 22 from the Teachers' Guide for your observations. On this occasion no prompting questions are provided to help you reach your conclusions.

17.6.2 FURTHER REACTIONS OF ARENES

HAZARD WARNING: *BROMINE IS HIGHLY CORROSIVE AND CAUSES PAINFUL BURNS.*
Keep a bottle of sodium thiosulphate close by to deal with any mishaps. IT IS BEST TO WEAR GLOVES.

Arenes undergo reactions involving the benzene ring under special conditions. These conditions vary according to the nature of other groups present on the ring. The methyl group in methylbenzene makes the ring slightly more reactive than that of benzene itself. Methoxybenzene is more reactive still and will be used in some of the subsequent tests. For this subsection use a copy of Table 23 from the Teachers' Guide.

ASSESSMENT: remember that a rise in temperature may indicate a chemical change is taking place. See the guidelines on organic observation and deduction exercises (1.3 and 1.4).

FURTHER STUDY PROBLEMS:

(1) Construct models of the compounds that you have used for your tests. If there is insufficient time during lessons, ask your teacher if you may use a model kit when you have a private study period. Examine the differences in the types of bond present. Refer to Table 30. Can you see any features which might explain the differences found in the reactions of alkanes, alkenes and arenes?

(2) Look carefully at some PEEL models if they are available. Can you suggest how a bromine molecule could become polarised when close to a carbon-carbon double bond? Once polarised, which end of the bromine is most likely to attack the alkene?

(3) A positively charged group which attacks a region of negative charge, **with the subsequent formation of a covalent bond,** is known as an **electrophile.** Similarly, a negatively charged group which attacks a region of positive charge, **with the subsequent formation of a covalent bond,** is known as a **nucleophile.** When bromine reacts with an alkene, is it behaving as an electrophile or a nucleophile? The reaction is an **addition** reaction.

(4) Study the PEEL model of benzene. If benzene undergoes an addition reaction, what happens to the delocalised π-electron system?

(5) Consider the observation you made when you treated methylbenzene with bromine and an iron nail (17.6.2) together with your answer to the previous question. What type of reaction do you think has occurred? Is it an addition or a substitution reaction?

(6) Using your results for exercises 17.2, 17.3 and 17.6 make a comparison of the properties of alkanes, alkenes and arenes. You may consider hexane, cyclohexene and methylbenzene to be typical of alkanes, alkenes and arenes respectively. Your comparison may be in essay form, or in a tabular form. Whichever presentation you use, you should include a brief introduction and a conclusion.

17.7 PREPARATION OF METHYL 3-NITROBENZOATE.

HAZARD WARNING: *CONCENTRATED NITRIC AND SULPHURIC ACIDS ARE CORROSIVE.*

As indicated in section 17.6, benzene is too hazardous to use in the school laboratory. However, the nitration of benzene to nitrobenzene is a reaction of considerable synthetic importance. Nitrobenzene and similar nitro compounds provide important intermediates in the manufacture of many important compounds from drugs to dyestuffs.

An ester of benzoic acid provides a suitable alternative to benzene for the preparation and purification of a nitro-aromatic compound. As the product is a solid it is easy to purify by recrystallisation from a suitable solvent. This experiment provides an introduction to this important purification technique. The equation for the reaction is:

ASSESSMENT: You may be assessed on your manipulative skills (1.7). You are reminded of the guidance in sections 2.5, 2.6 and 2.7 concerning recrystallisation, use of a Buchner funnel and the determination of a melting point respectively. At the end of the practical you should hand in your product, together with your report on the experiment. This should include the calculation of your percentage yield and the melting point of your sample.

PROCEDURE:

(1) The nitrating mixture: measure 2 cm^3 of concentrated nitric acid into a hard glass test tube. Add 2 cm^3 of concentrated sulphuric acid dropwise to the nitric acid. Make sure that you mix the two acids. *TAKE CARE!*

(2) Measure 6 cm^3 of concentrated sulphuric acid into a hard glass test tube (this acid provides a solvent for the ester). Place this tube, together with the test tube containing the nitrating mixture into a beaker of crushed ice. It is important that the reaction mixture is kept at or below about 10 °C throughout the reaction. At higher temperatures, disubstitution occurs.

(3) Weigh (to the nearest 0.1 g) about 3 cm^3 of methyl benzoate into a 100 cm^3 conical flask. Record this mass for your calculation of percentage yield.

(4) Check that your concentrated acids have cooled to below 10 °C. Add the 6 cm^3 portion of the concentrated sulphuric acid to the ester in the flask and place the flask in the beaker of ice.

(5) Using a dropping pipette, add the nitrating mixture a few drops at a time to the ester solution in the flask. Stir the mixture gently with the thermometer and try to keep the mixture cool. The addition of the nitrating mixture will take 15 to 20 minutes.

(6) On completing the addition, leave the mixture to stand at room temperature for a further 15 minutes.

(7) Now pour the mixture on to about 30 cm^3 of crushed ice in a 100 cm^3 beaker. This is a good point to leave the mixture until the next lesson if you are unable to complete the preparation in one go.

(8) When the ice has melted, filter the mixture using a small (e.g. 5.5 cm) Buchner funnel. Wash the solid well with at least three 10 cm^3 portions of water. Using the filter pump, draw air over the solid to remove as much water as possible.

(9) Heat a small quantity of ethanol (industrial methylated spirits) in a conical flask on a water bath. Keep the hot ethanol away from naked flames. You could share a flask of ethanol with your neighbour (50 cm^3 should be plenty for both of you).

(10) Transfer your solid product to a clean, dry 100 cm^3 conical flask. Add sufficient hot ethanol to just dissolve the solid. You will need to warm the solution in the hot water bath as you do this. You should obtain a clear liquid.

(11) Leave the solution to cool. Crystals of methyl 3-nitrobenzoate should separate. Filter these off when the solution is quite cool. Dry your product in air, covered with a filter paper.

(12) Weigh your dried product and record your yield in grams. Calculate the percentage yield, based on the mass of ester used at the start. Place your product in a sample tube labelled with the name of the product and your name.

(13) Determine the range of melting of your sample and record this in your report. Pure methyl 3-nitrobenzoate melts at 78 °C.

17.8 THE IDENTIFICATION OF THREE UNKNOWN HYDROCARBONS.

You are provided with a few cm^3 of each of three unlabelled liquid hydrocarbons. One of these is an alkane, one an alkene and the third an arene.

Devise a series of test tube reactions which would establish which is which. You may use any of the reagents you met in experiments 17.2, 17.4 or 17.6. You must give a positive test for each, it will NOT be acceptable to identify the third compound by elimination.

ASSESSMENT: You will be given credit for a concise yet complete scheme. Be sure to give full instructions on how you carry out each test and the results that might be obtained, and show how these would be interpreted. You may present your scheme in whatever form you feel is most appropriate. This could be in a tabular form or as a flow chart.

18. ALCOHOLS AND PHENOL

18.1 Introduction.
18.2 Properties of ethanol.
18.3 Oxidation of primary, secondary and tertiary alcohols.
18.4 The preparations of ethanal and ethanoic acid.
18.5 The preparation of ethyl ethanoate.
18.6 Preparation of bromoethane.
18.7 The dehydration of ethanol.
18.8 Properties of phenol.

18.1 INTRODUCTION.

AIM: the aim of this topic is to investigate the typical physical and chemical properties of some of the compounds containing the hydroxyl functional group (-OH). The effect of the hydrocarbon part of the molecule on the behaviour of the hydroxyl group will also be investigated.

THEORY: Compounds containing the hydroxyl group include:

  aliphatic alcohols
  aromatic alcohols (phenols)
  carboxylic acids
  carbohydrates.

Aliphatic alcohols may be divided into three further types, with the structures shown in Table 31.

	primary -CH$_2$OH	secondary >CHOH	tertiary ->COH
Number of C–C bonds to adjacent carbon atoms	1	2	3
Example	CH$_3$CH$_2$OH	(CH$_3$)$_2$CHOH	(CH$_3$)$_3$COH

Table 31: The Structures of Aliphatic Alcohols.

The hydroxyl group in carboxylic acids is strongly influenced by the neighbouring carbonyl group >C=O which makes the hydroxyl group acidic. For this reason it will be studied in a later topic.

The reactions of alcohols may be understood by considering both bond polarities and bond energies. The latter are given in Table 32.

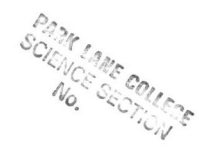

Bond	Bond Energy /kJ mol⁻¹
C–C	347
C–H	413
C–O	358
O–H	464

Table 32: Some Bond Energies.

SUMMARY: At the end of this topic you should know

(1) how the –OH group affects the physical properties in comparison to other simple organic compounds of similar molecular mass,

(2) how the hydrocarbon part of the molecule affects the reactions of the hydroxyl group,

(3) which bonds break most readily, C–H, C–C, C–O or O–H, and whether they break homo- or heterolytically,

(4) how the nature of the attacking reagent often determines which bond breaks,

(5) how primary, secondary and tertiary alcohols may be distinguished by test tube reactions,

(6) how change of reaction conditions can influence the nature of the products (with regard to oxidation or dehydration of a primary alcohol),

(7) know what is meant by an elimination reaction and have met more examples of substitution reactions; know what is meant by a nucleophile,

(8) have gained experience in planning syntheses and acquired more skill in preparative organic chemistry.

LINKS: This a particularly important topic and you should be thoroughly conversant with the reactions introduced before you start the topics on aldehydes and ketones or on carboxylic acids. Be sure that you compare the reactivity of the benzene ring in phenol with that of the other aromatic hydrocarbons met in Topic 17. The preparation of ethyl ethanoate puts into practice some of the concepts met in Topic 7 on equilibria and Topic 9 on rates.

18.2 PROPERTIES OF ETHANOL.

PREPARATION FOR THIS PRACTICAL: Answer the following questions before you start the practical work.

(1) Water can act as an acid or a base because of its ability to lose or gain protons. Could ethanol also behave as an acid or a base? If you think it could, write equations to show how it might do so.

(2) Draw diagrams to show the polarities of the C–O and O–H bonds in ethanol. Use δ+ and δ– to show the positive and negative ends of each bond.

(3) Look at Table 32 and decide which of the two bonds, C–O or O–H, is more likely to break. When either of these bonds are broken, will the fission be homo- or heterolytic?

(4) At which atom in ethanol might you expect reaction to occur with an electrophile?

(5) What sort of reagent might attack the carbon atom of the C–O bond?

HAZARD WARNINGS: ETHANOL INFLAMMABLE.
                    GLACIAL ETHANOIC AND CONCENTRATED SULPHURIC ACIDS
                    ARE CORROSIVE.

RESIDUE DISPOSAL: POUR ALL RESIDUES AFTER COOLING INTO
                    RUNNING WATER IN FUME CUPBOARD SINK.

ASSESSMENT: See the guidelines on organic test tube observation and deduction exercise (see 1.2, 1.3 and 1.4).

Use a copy of Table 24 from the Teachers' Guide for your results. You will need these results later for comparison with those obtained using phenol (18.8).

18.3 OXIDATION OF PRIMARY, SECONDARY AND TERTIARY ALCOHOLS.

ASSESSMENT: Again the general guidelines on organic test tube observation and deduction exercises apply (see 1.2, 1.3 and 1.4). Note particularly the advice on the detection of odours (1.3).

You are provided with five alcohols, propan-1-ol, propan-2-ol, 2-methylpropan-2-ol and two unknown alcohols labelled A and B.

Acidify about 2 cm³ of aqueous potassium dichromate(VI) with an equal volume of dilute sulphuric acid, add 2-3 drops of one of the three named alcohols. Warm the mixture gently, then boil. Note changes in odour and check the acidity of the vapour with blue litmus paper. Repeat the test with the other two named alcohols.

Draw up a table to present your observations and conclusions. In your table draw the structural formula and state the type (i.e. primary etc) of each alcohol. In each case deduce whether oxidation has taken place. Try to name the organic products formed.

If you have time repeat the test with the two unknown alcohols A and B. Try to classify these as primary, secondary or tertiary.

18.4 THE PREPARATIONS OF ETHANAL AND ETHANOIC ACID.

You are required to plan two preparative experiments. You are provided with ethanol, sulphuric acid (dilute or concentrated), solid sodium dichromate(VI) and glassware of the type (interchangeable joints) that you have used in other preparative experiments. You also have access to other apparatus in the laboratory.

You are NOT required to purify your products, although they must be separated from the mixture used in the reaction by some means. You may consult other experiments in your practical folder and a data book but NOT other practical textbooks.

Your plan must give an indication of quantities to be used and details of apparatus to set up (with appropriate diagrams). Reasons for your choice of reagents, conditions and apparatus selected must also be given. You should be careful to specify the length of time required for heating your reaction mixtures (see 18.2).

You may find the balanced equations for the reactions helpful:

(a) for the preparation of ethanal:

$$3CH_3CH_2OH + Cr_2O_7^{2-} + 8H^+ \rightarrow 3CH_3CHO + 2Cr^{3+} + 7H_2O$$

(b) for the preparation of ethanoic acid:

$$3CH_3CH_2OH + 2Cr_2O_7^{2-} + 16H^+ \rightarrow 3CH_3CO_2H + 4Cr^{3+} + 11H_2O$$

After your teacher has seen your plan you may, if time permits, be able to prepare one (or even both) of the required products, following your suggested method. At this stage, you may find that you wish to modify your plan in the light of your experience.

ASSESSMENT: You may be assessed on your planning skills (1.6). Section 2.4 on the use of apparatus with ground glass joints may be useful. Your teacher will wish to see the following in your plan:

(1)   An awareness of the need for the control of quantities and conditions to produce the desired products,

(2)   A clear account giving the procedure that could be followed by another A-level student.

If subsequently you are able to carry out your plan, your teachers will note whether you are capable of modifying it, if necessary, during the course of your practical work. They will assist you if you request help but otherwise may step in only if they see that you are likely to do something dangerous.

18.5 THE PREPARATION OF ETHYL ETHANOATE

This is an example of an esterification reaction, in this case between ethanol and ethanoic acid. You have already met the reaction on a test tube scale in 18.2 test (c).

$$C_2H_5OH + CH_3CO_2H \rightarrow CH_3CO_2C_2H_5 + H_2O$$

An acid catalyst is required. After a period of reflux an equilibrium mixture is obtained with a good proportion of the reagents still present.

ASSESSMENT: You may be assessed on your manipulative skills (1.7). Section 2.4 on the use of apparatus with ground glass joints may be useful as well as section 2.8 on the use of the separating funnel. At the end of this practical you should hand in your written report of the experiment, together with your sample.

PROCEDURE: Place 15 cm^3 of ethanol and 8 cm^3 of glacial ethanoic acid in a 50 cm^3 pear shaped flask. Slowly add 5 cm^3 of concentrated sulphuric acid. Mix well and cool the flask in cold water during this addition.

Fit the flask with a condenser for reflux and place in a water bath. Add a boiling chip to the contents of the flask. Raise the temperature of the water bath to the point where the flask contents begin to boil. Reflux the mixture gently for about 30 minutes.

At the end of this time cool the mixture and rearrange the apparatus for distillation. The flask may be heated directly over a gauze using a small flame. A thermometer is not needed. Collect the first 12 cm^3 of distillate. Stop distilling if there are signs of a gas being evolved in the flask. After the distillation wash and dry your apparatus ready for the final distillation.

To purify the product, use a small (25 cm^3) separating funnel and wash the distillate with about 5 cm^3 of saturated aqueous calcium chloride. This removes any ethanol present. Separate the upper, ester layer from the aqueous calcium chloride and wash the ester with about 5 cm^3 of dilute sodium carbonate. Keep the upper layer of ester and wash with about 5 cm^3 of water. Transfer the upper layer to a small conical flask or test tube and add anhydrous calcium chloride. Leave to dry, then filter through a small plug of glass wool into a clean dry pear shaped flask. Arrange the apparatus for distillation again. Redistil, collecting the fraction that boils between 75 and 79 °C. Weigh your sample and calculate the percentage yield. Put your sample in a labelled tube and hand in with your report. Answer the following questions in your written report:

(1)   Why do you think a catalyst is needed in this reaction?

(2)   Give **two** reasons for refluxing the mixture for thirty minutes.

(3)   What will be the effect of the reflux temperature on the yield of ester?

(4)   Look up the densities of ethanol and glacial ethanoic acid. Calculate the amounts of each used in the reaction mixture (in moles). Explain why equimolar amounts were not used.

(5) Assuming the reaction could go to completion, calculate the theoretical yield of ester.

(6) Name other possible organic byproducts from the reaction mixture.

(7) Why is the impure ester washed with aqueous sodium carbonate?

18.6 PREPARATION OF BROMOETHANE.

HAZARD WARNING: CONCENTRATED SULPHURIC ACID CORROSIVE.
BROMOETHANE VAPOUR HARMFUL.

DISPOSAL: COOL REACTION MIXTURE AND POUR INTO COLD WATER
IN FUME CUPBOARD SINK.

This preparation illustrates the nucleophilic substitution of an hydroxyl group by a halogen atom. This type of reaction was met on a test tube scale in Experiment 18.2(d). A small sample of bromoethane is prepared but the sample is not purified.

The equation for the reaction is:

$$C_2H_5OH + HBr \rightarrow C_2H_5Br + H_2O$$

The substitution is easily reversed and requires the use of concentrated sulphuric acid and potassium bromide to produce the hydrogen bromide. The ethanol is included in the reaction mixture. Heating causes the product to distil and a small sample may be collected under water.

ASSESSMENT: You may be assessed on your manipulative skills (1.7). Your teacher will assess your organisation and the care with which you carry out the experiment.

PROCEDURE:

(1) Carefully add 5 cm³ of concentrated sulphuric acid to 5 cm³ of ethanol in a hard glass boiling tube. Add a little of the acid at a time, mix thoroughly and cool the tube in cold water.

(2) Now add about 6 g of potassium bromide and insert the delivery tube. Arrange the apparatus as shown in figure 15.

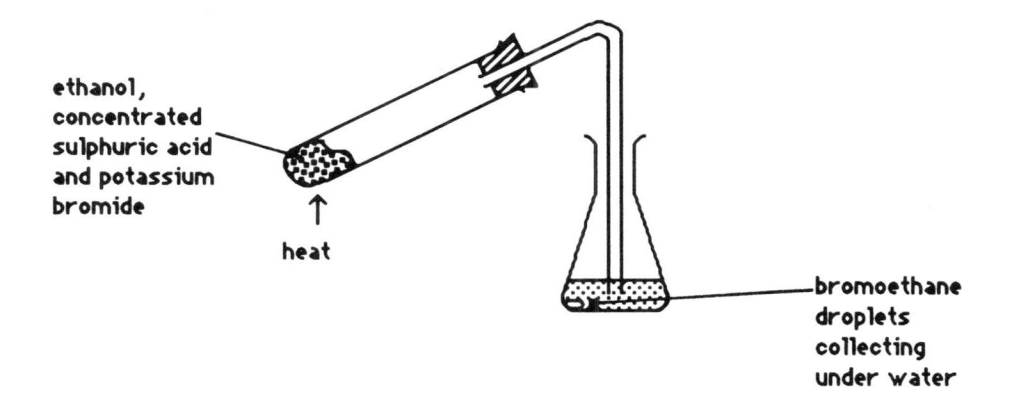

Figure 15: The Preparation of Bromoethane.

(3) Gently heat the mixture over a small flame. The vapours dissolve or condense in the cold water in the conical flask.

(4) Continue heating until a few oily droplets of bromoethane collect under the water. Remove the delivery tube from the water before removing the flame from the boiling tube.

After you have completed the preparation, answer the following questions:

(1) Explain in terms of intermolecular forces why the bromoethane does not dissolve in the water.

(2) What other reactions might occur if the mixture of ethanol and concentrated sulphuric acid is not kept cool as it is prepared? Write balanced equations for these reactions and name the possible products.

(3) What compound dissolves in the water in the conical flask?

(4) Outline how you might purify a sample of bromoethane obtained using this reaction.

18.7 THE DEHYDRATION OF ETHANOL.

This reaction is an example of an elimination reaction. It was met in Experiment 18.2(d)(ii) on a test tube scale using concentrated sulphuric acid. In this preparation, a small sample of ethanol is dehydrated using hot pumice as a surface on which the ethanol molecule may be cracked.

ASSESSMENT: You may be assessed on your manipulative skills (1.7). Your teacher will watch how you organise your work and assess the care with which you carry out the experiment.

PROCEDURE:

(1) Place a tuft of mineral wool in the bottom of a hard glass boiling tube.

(2) Soak the wool in ethanol (use industrial methylated spirits).

(3) Place a few spatula measures of pumice in the boiling tube as shown in Figure 16.

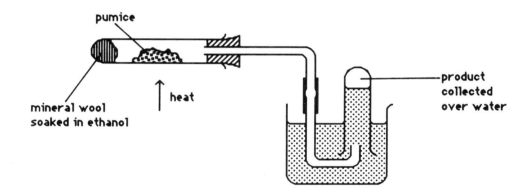

Figure 16: Dehydration of Ethanol.

(4) Clamp the boiling tube in a horizontal position and connect to a delivery tube as shown.

(5) Fill three or four test tubes with water and place ready to collect the gas produced.

(6) Heat the boiling tube below the pumice. Occasionally play the flame over the mineral wool to provide a slow stream of ethanol vapour. Take care to prevent water sucking back via the delivery tube.

(7) When you have collected several tubes of gas, disconnect the delivery tube before removing the bunsen flame.

(8) Carry out three simple tests to identify the product. Describe the tests and your observations.

(9) Write an equation for the reaction which has occurred.

114

18.8 PROPERTIES OF PHENOL.

HAZARD WARNING: *PHENOL IS BOTH TOXIC AND CORROSIVE. Handle it with care, it can produce painful burns and is absorbed through the skin. WASH AWAY ANY SPILT CRYSTALS WITH PLENTY OF WATER, WEAR GLOVES IF POSSIBLE.*

RESIDUE DISPOSAL: *WASH ALL THE RESIDUES AWAY WITH WATER IN THE FUME CUPBOARD SINK.*

Use a copy of Table 25 from the Teachers' Guide. Answer the questions in the spaces provided. The structure of phenol is:

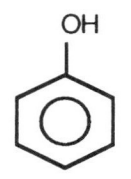

FURTHER STUDY QUESTIONS:

(1)   Compare the reactions of phenol with those of ethanol. Can you suggest any reason for the observed differences in acidity of phenol and ethanol?

(2)   Compare the reactivity of the benzene ring in phenol with that of the benzene ring in other arenes (see 17.6).

19. ALDEHYDES AND KETONES

19.1 Introduction.
19.2 Reactions of aldehydes and ketones.
19.3 Preparation of propanone from propan-2-ol.

19.1 INTRODUCTION.

AIM: In this topic you will investigate the chemical reactions of aldehydes and ketones. You will also prepare a sample of a ketone by oxidation of a secondary alcohol as well as reducing a different ketone to its corresponding secondary alcohol.

THEORY: Aldehydes and ketones both contain the carbonyl group, $>C=O$. In aldehydes this group is joined to a carbon and to a hydrogen (it is often written as -CHO). In ketones it is joined to two carbons.

$$\text{e.g. propanal, } CH_3CH_2CHO; \text{ propanone, } (CH_3)_2CO$$

Aldehydes have names which end in -al whilst ketones have names which end in -one. These are prefixed by the name of the parent hydrocarbon without the final -e. An exception to this naming system that you will meet is benzaldehyde, C_6H_5CHO.

It is the carbonyl group which characterises the reactions of aldehydes and ketones. Like the carbon-carbon double bond, the carbonyl double bond undergoes addition reactions. Bond energy data are given in Table 33. These show that the C–O π-bond is about as strong as the C–O σ-bond. As the C–C π-bond is weaker than the C–C σ-bond, we would not expect addition reactions to occur so easily to $>C=O$ as we found it did to $>C=C<$. However, addition to $>C=O$ is strongly influenced by its polarity.

Bond	Bond Energy /kJ mol^{-1}
C–C	+347
C=C	+612
C–O	+358
C=O	+736 (aldehydes) +749 (ketones)

Table 33: Bond energy data.

Both aldehydes and ketones can be reduced to their corresponding alcohols. It should be remembered (Topic 18) that aldehydes are formed by oxidation of primary alcohols under mild conditions e.g.

$$CH_3CH_2OH + [O] \rightarrow CH_3CHO + H_2O$$

Ketones are produced by oxidation of secondary alcohols e.g.

$$(CH_3)_2CHOH + [O] \rightarrow (CH_3)_2CO + H_2O$$

However aldehydes, unlike ketones, may be oxidised further to carboxylic acids:

$$CH_3CHO + [O] \rightarrow CH_3COOH$$

This requires an excess of the oxidising agent and more vigorous conditions, typically longer refluxing in an excess of acidified dichromate (see 18.4).

SUMMARY: At the end of this topic you should:

(1)   know that the formation of a yellow or orange precipitate with 2,4-dinitrophenylhydrazine shows the presence of an aldehyde or ketone carbonyl group,

(2)   understand what is meant by the term condensation reaction,

(3)   know the different ways in which aldehydes may be oxidised to carboxylic acids and how the results of such oxidation reactions enable aldehydes to be distinguished from ketones,

(4)   have gained a stronger appreciation of the reactions of alcohols through the reactions of aldehydes and ketones.

LINKS: As both aldehydes and ketones are obtained by oxidation of alcohols you should revise Topic 18 on alcohols before you start the practical work in this topic.

19.2 REACTIONS OF ALDEHYDES AND KETONES.

In this practical you will carry out a series of test tube reactions on both aliphatic and aromatic aldehydes and ketones. The compounds you will use are ethanal, propanone, benzaldehyde and phenylethanone:

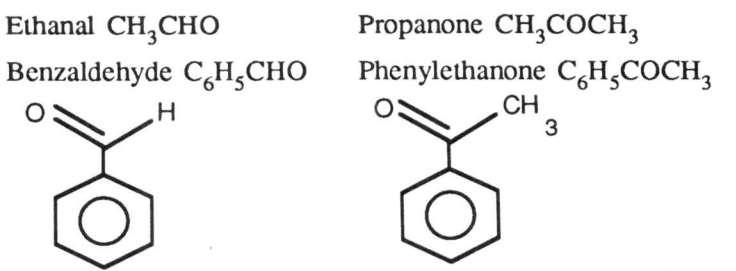

Ethanal CH_3CHO Propanone CH_3COCH_3

Benzaldehyde C_6H_5CHO Phenylethanone $C_6H_5COCH_3$

ASSESSMENT: See the guidelines on test tube observation and deduction exercises (1.2, 1.3 and 1.4).

Use copies of Tables 26 and 27 from the Teachers' Guide for this practical. Table 26 is for the alphatic compounds, whilst Table 27 is for the aromatic compounds. You will see that the tests are the same in the two tables, with the exception of the additional test (d)(iv) using acidified manganate(VII) for the aromatic compounds. It is a good idea to carry out the same test for all four compounds at the same time. Brady's reagent is a dilute solution of 2,4-dinitrophenylhydrazine:

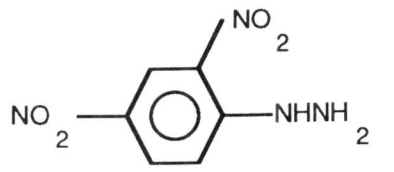

When you have finished the tests, answer the following questions.

QUESTIONS:

(1)   What is the polarity of the carbonyl group? When a carbonyl group undergoes an addition reaction, the first covalent bond is formed to the carbon of the >C=O. Is the attacking species an electrophile or a nucleophile? How does this compare to addition to alkenes?

(2)   The solubility of carbonyl compounds in water could be helped if an addition reaction occurred with water. Draw the structure of a possible addition product between ethanal and water. What other type of interaction will increase the solubility?

(3)   Do the four compounds all produce yellow or orange precipitates with Brady's reagent? What group is common to all four compounds which could give rise to a common reaction?

In this reaction a water molecule is eliminated. The reaction is known as a condensation. (In fact the mechanism involves an addition followed by an elimination.) Use your textbook or notes to help you write a balanced equation for each of the reactions observed with Brady's reagent.

(4) Which of the four compounds are oxidised by acidified dichromate? Name the organic oxidation products and write balanced equations for the reactions involved.

(5) Which compounds give a silver mirror with Tollen's reagent?

(6) Which compounds reduce Fehling's solution?

(7) Could either Tollen's reagent or Fehling's solution be used to distinguish between an aldehyde and a ketone?

(8) Name the organic product(s) formed when acidified manganate (VII) is used to oxidise the aromatic compounds. Write balanced equation(s) for the reactions observed.

(9) Which group is responsible for the formation of triiodomethane in test (e)?

19.3 PREPARATION OF PROPANONE FROM PROPAN-2-OL.

This preparation illustrates the oxidation of a secondary alcohol to a ketone. In Topic 18, you planned an experiment to oxidise a primary alcohol to an aldehyde and to a carboxylic acid (Experiment 18.4).

ASSESSMENT: Refer to the use of apparatus with ground glass joints (2.4). At the end of the experiment hand in a sample of your product in a labelled sample tube.

PROCEDURE:

(1) Carefully add 3 cm^3 of concentrated sulphuric acid dropwise to 8 cm^3 of distilled water in a 50 cm^3 pear-shaped flask. Cool the mixture and then add 8.0 g of sodium dichromate. Swirl the contents of the flask to dissolve the dichromate.

(2) Assemble the flask for distillation, placing a tap funnel in the still head instead of a thermometer (see figure 15, topic 17).

(3) Place 6 cm^3 of propan-2-ol in the tap funnel.

(4) Warm the contents of the flask on a water bath at about 60 °C.

(5) Add the propan-2-ol dropwise to the oxidising mixture in the flask.

(6) The propanone should distil over as it is formed. If it does not, complete the addition and then raise the temperature of the water bath until the propanone distils steadily. Collect about 5 cm^3 of impure product.

(7) Check that you have oxidised the alcohol by adding Brady's reagent to a sample of your propanone. Record your observation in your report.

(8) Test a second portion of your product by boiling it with Fehling's solution. What does the result of this test tell you? Record your result and conclusion in your report.

(9) Compare the odour of your product with the odour of the propanone in the laboratory reagent bottle.

(10) Write a balanced equation for the reaction in your report.

20. ORGANIC HALOGEN COMPOUNDS

20.1 Introduction.
20.2 The hydrolysis of organic chlorine compounds.
20.3 Investigating the hydrolysis of a bromoalkane.
20.4 The synthesis of a herbicide.

20.1 INTRODUCTION.

AIM: The topic enables you to study the effects of different organic structures on the rate of hydrolysis of the carbon–chlorine (C–Cl) and carbon–bromine (C–Br) bonds. An extended preparation of a herbicide is also included to enable you to gain a better appreciation of synthesis in an industrial or higher educational laboratory. The synthesis of this compound is followed by an examination of its stability in soil in order to illustrate one way in which chemists examine the environmental acceptability of such a compound.

THEORY: Hydrolysis. In your study of Organic Chemistry, you will have become aware of the way in which different hydrocarbon groups affect the reactivity of functional groups. Organic halogen compounds show a marked change in their behaviour towards their reaction with water (with the exception of organic fluorine compounds which do not hydrolyse). A general equation for this hydrolysis reaction is:

$$RX(l) + H_2O(l) \rightarrow ROH(aq) + HX(aq)$$

where R = an alkyl, aryl or acyl group.

Changes in reactivity are sufficiently marked for differences in the rates of hydrolysis of organic chlorine compounds and of bromobutane isomers to be observed. The reaction is a nucleophilic substitution, the nucleophile may be water or hydroxide ion.

Organic Synthesis. Many organic halogen compounds have important uses. Examples include dichloromethane as a solvent and degreasing agent, bromochlorodifluoromethane as a fire extinguishing fluid (BCF) and fluothane as an anaesthetic. However many other organic chlorine and organic bromine compounds are especially important as intermediates in the synthesis of other products from drugs to agricultural chemicals. The synthesis of a herbicide provides an example of an organic chlorine compound being used as an intermediate.

SUMMARY: At the end of this topic you should:

(1) know the conditions required for the hydrolysis of different types of organic chlorine compound and be able to write equations for the reactions concerned,

(2) be able to explain the relative rates of hydrolysis of organic chlorine compounds in terms of the structures of the compounds,

(3) have developed a better understanding of the experimental methods for studying the rates of reaction and of the use of the rate equation in helping to establish the reaction mechanism,

(4) gained an understanding of the techniques involved in a longer chemical synthesis and of the value of organic chlorine compounds as intermediates in producing many important compounds.

LINKS: Reactions in which organic chlorine compounds are formed appear in Topics 18 and 21. You will have studied Topic 9 on Rates of Reaction before you start some of the work in this Topic.

119

20.2 THE HYDROLYSIS OF ORGANIC CHLORINE COMPOUNDS.

HAZARD WARNING: *ETHANOYL CHLORIDE REACTS VIOLENTLY WITH WATER, IT IS ALSO CORROSIVE.*
AVOID INHALING VAPOURS OF ORGANIC CHLORINE COMPOUNDS.

In this practical you will compare the relative rates of hydrolysis of the following compounds:

* 1-chlorobutane
* chlorobenzene
* chloromethylbenzene
* ethanoyl chloride

ASSESSMENT: You may be assessed on the interpretation of your results (1.4).

PROCEDURE:

(1)   Prepare about 4 cm^3 of a mixture containing equal volumes of 0.025 mol dm^{-3} silver nitrate and ethanol. Divide this into four portions.

(2)   Take one of the portions of aqueous ethanolic silver nitrate and add a few drops of ethanoyl chloride. Note the time taken to produce a white precipitate.

(3)   Treat another portion of the silver nitrate with a few drops of 1-chlorobutane, a third with a few drops of chlorobenzene and the fourth portion with chloromethylbenzene. Place these three tubes in a water bath at 60 °C and note the time taken for a white precipitate to form.

(4)   If any tube fails to produce a white precipitate within fifteen minutes, try raising the temperature of the water bath to 100 °C.

Now answer the following questions:

(1)   What is the white precipitate which forms with the silver nitrate? Write an equation for its formation.

(2)   Why is ethanol included in the reaction mixture?

(3)   Place the compounds in order of increasing rate of formation of this precipitate.

(4)   Draw the graphic display (i.e. full structural) formulae of the four organic chlorine compounds.

(5)   Explain the trend you have observed by considering how the organic part of each compound influences the polarity of the carbon-chlorine bond.

20.3 INVESTIGATING THE HYDROLYSIS OF A BROMOALKANE.

1-Bromobutane hydrolyses very slowly in water at room temperature. Even when hydroxide ion is used as the nucleophile and the temperature is raised, hydrolysis takes several days.

However, 2-bromo-2-methylpropane hydrolyses much more rapidly in **water** at room temperature.

The mechanism of the hydrolysis of these two isomers is in fact different, one being a first order reaction, the other second order. The purpose of this practical is to establish which is which by means of an experiment to determine the overall order of the reaction involving the 2-bromo-2-methylpropane.

ASSESSMENT: You may be assessed on your skills in designing an experiment (1.6).

PROCEDURE:

(1)   You are provided with the following:

* a 1 cm^3 sample of 2-bromo-2-methylpropane
* ethanol
* a standardised solution of 0.100 mol dm^{-3} sodium hydroxide
* a pH meter and pH electrode
* a conductivity meter
* the usual range of laboratory glassware
* de-ionised or distilled water
* crushed ice

(2)   Design an experiment using some of these materials to determine the rate equation for the hydrolysis of the 2-bromo-2-methylpropane. Your plan should be presented in such a way that it could be followed successfully by another A-level student.

(3)   Carry out your experiment and determine the overall order of reaction.

(4)   Suggest a possible mechanism for the hydrolysis of the 2-bromo-2-methylpropane.

(5)   Bearing in mind that the overall order for the hydrolysis of 1-bromobutane is different from that of the 2-bromo-2-methylpropane (see above), suggest a mechanism for the hydrolysis of the 1-bromobutane.

20.4 THE SYNTHESIS OF A HERBICIDE.

The herbicide 2,4-D has been in use for about forty years. It is often found in lawn weedkillers produced for use in gardens. It is used to kill broad-leaved weeds in grass or cereal crops. Its structure is similar to that of a growth hormone and it works by interfering with the growth processes of broad-leaved plants so that they wither and die. The preparation of 2,4-D involves the reaction of 2,4-dichlorophenol with chloroethanoic acid. This produces 2,4-D as the acid. It is often used as a salt but it may also be used as an ester. We shall convert it to its methyl ester.

ASSESSMENT: In the following subsections you may be assessed on your manipulative skills (1.7).

20.4.1 PREPARATION OF 2,4-D ACID.

HAZARD WARNING: *BOTH 2,4-DICHLOROPHENOL AND CHLOROETHANOIC ACID ARE HARMFUL AND CORROSIVE. THEY CAUSE BURNS.*

ETHOXYETHANE IS <u>HIGHLY</u> INFLAMMABLE, EXTINGUISH ALL FLAMES IN THE LABORATORY DURING USE.

RESIDUE DISPOSAL: *WASH WITH PLENTY OF RUNNING WATER. LEAVE ETHOXYETHANE RESIDUES IN A LABELLED BEAKER IN FUME CUPBOARD.*

2,4-Dichlorophenol is dissolved in sodium hydroxide. The solution is then refluxed with chloroethanoic acid. The product is extracted as the sodium salt; this enables unreacted phenol to be washed away in ethoxyethane. The acid is then regenerated by treatment of the sodium salt with an excess of hydrochloric acid.

During the reflux stage of the preparation answer the following questions:

(1)   Draw the displayed formulae of 2,4-dichlorophenol and of chloroethanoic acid.

(2)   How might the phenol react with sodium hydroxide? Write an equation for the reaction involved.

(3)   In the reaction with chloroethanoic acid, the chlorine atom is replaced by the organic ion from the reaction of the phenol and sodium hydroxide. What is the name given to this type of reaction? What is the name given to the type of reagent represented by the organic ion?

(4)   Draw the displayed formula of the product of the reaction with chloroethanoic acid (i.e. of 2,4-D acid). Write a balanced equation for the reaction involved.

(5)   Why should sodium carbonate produce the sodium salt of the 2,4-D acid but not that of the 2,4-dichlorophenol?

PROCEDURE:

(1)   Weigh 2.2 g of sodium hydroxide pellets (CARE) and dissolve these in 15 cm^3 of distilled water.

(2)   Carefully weigh 4.1 g of 2,4-dichlorophenol. If it has set solid, it may be necessary to stand the bottle in warm water to melt it (melting point 41-44 °C). Dissolve this sample in the solution of sodium hydroxide from (1).

(3)   Place the alkaline solution of the phenol in a 50 cm^3 pear shaped flask and add 2.4 g of chloroethanoic acid. Fit the flask with a condenser and gently reflux the mixture over a gauze for one hour. Allow the mixture to cool.

(4)   Dissolve the solid produced in 100 cm^3 of near boiling distilled water. Cool this solution and then add 5 cm^3 of concentrated hydrochloric acid with stirring. Continue cooling in an ice bath when any oil should solidify. Filter the solid using a Buchner filter.

(5)   Dissolve the product in 25 cm^3 of ethoxyethane. There should be NO FLAMES in the laboratory!!! Add 50 cm^3 of dilute aqueous sodium carbonate to the ethereal solution and filter the white solid. This is the sodium salt of 2,4-D acid, any unreacted phenol is removed in the ether.

(6)   Dissolve this solid in 30 cm^3 of near boiling water, cool in an ice bath and add 5 cm^3 of concentrated hydrochloric acid to reprecipitate the 2,4-D as the acid. Filter, suck dry and place in a warm oven to complete the drying.

(7)   Weigh your dried sample, determine the percentage yield and melting point. The pure acid melts at 136-138 °C.

Your product is now ready to convert to an ester.

20.4.2 PREPARATION OF 2,4-D METHYL ESTER.

HAZARD WARNING: *ETHOXYETHANE AND METHANOL INFLAMMABLE.*
                      METHANOL IS TOXIC.

RESIDUE DISPOSAL: *LEAVE ETHOXYETHANE RESIDUES IN A LABELLED*
                      BEAKER IN FUME CUPBOARD.

In this stage the 2,4-D acid is converted to its methyl ester. Hydrochloric acid is used as the strong acid catalyst.

During the reflux stage of this preparation, write an equation for the formation of this ester and draw a displayed formula for the ester.

PROCEDURE:

(1) *WORKING IN A FUME CUPBOARD* place 2.0 g of 2,4-D acid in a dry 50 cm³ pear shaped flask and add 25 cm³ of methanol which has been saturated with hydrogen chloride.

(2) Attach a reflux condenser and reflux the mixture gently over a gauze for one hour. At the end of this time, extinguish the bunsen and rearrange the apparatus for distillation. Distil off the methanol at 66-75 °C. You will be left with an oil and a little water.

(3) Cool the residue thoroughly and add 25 cm³ ethoxyethane. There should be *NO FLAMES* in the laboratory. Using a separating funnel, wash the ether extract once with 10 cm³ of saturated sodium chloride, once with 10 cm³ of dilute aqueous sodium hydrogencarbonate and finally with a second 10 cm³ portion of the saturated sodium chloride. Discard each of these washings, the ether forms the upper layer in the separating funnel.

(4) Place the ether extract in a small conical flask and add a little anhydrous magnesium sulphate to dry the extract. Stopper the conical flask.

(5) Filter the dry extract through a glass wool plug into a clean, dry 50 cm³ pear shaped flask. Arrange the flask for distillation and distil off the ether using a bath of very hot water from the tap. *DO NOT USE A BUNSEN BURNER!!!*

The oily residue is the ester.

FOLLOW-UP QUESTION: Using a catalogue, look up the costs of all of your materials for the two stages of this preparation and calculate the cost of producing your small sample.

21. CARBOXYLIC ACIDS AND THEIR DERIVATIVES

21.1 Introduction to carboxylic acids and their derivatives.
21.2 Properties of carboxylic acids.
21.3 The hydrolysis of an ester.
21.4 Acid chlorides and anhydrides.
21.5 Preparation of phenyl benzoate.
21.6 Preparation of aspirin.

21.1 INTRODUCTION TO CARBOXYLIC ACIDS AND THEIR DERIVATIVES.

AIMS: In this topic you will be introduced to the variety of reactions of the carboxylic acid functional group and of the derivatives of the carboxylic acids.

THEORY: The carboxylic acid functional group combines the carbonyl group with the hydroxyl group. This combination of groups produces some significant differences in behaviour in comparison to alcohols or aldehydes and ketones.

Acid behaviour. Most carboxylic acids are weak acids, ionising in water to produce carboxylate ions. These ions are stabilised by delocalisation of the carbonyl π-bond and the negative charge over the carbon and two oxygen atoms.

$$CH_3CO_2H(aq) \rightleftharpoons CH_3CO_2^-(aq) + H^+$$

Carboxylic acids react readily with alkalis and with bases to form a range of salts.

Reactivity of Carbonyl Carbon. The two oxygen atoms produce a positive charge on this carbon atom. Hence it will be open to attack by nucleophiles.

Derivatives include esters, acid chlorides and anhydrides and amides.

SUMMARY: At the end of this topic you should:

(1)   be familiar with the reactions of carboxylic acids and their derivatives,

(2)   have gained some more skill in the synthesis of organic compounds as well as making some compounds of interest.

LINKS: There are important links between the chemistry of primary alcohols (Topic 18), aldehydes (Topic 19) and carboxylic acids. You will also meet some organic nitrogen compounds for the first time. These are studied in more detail in Topic 22.

21.2 PROPERTIES OF CARBOXYLIC ACIDS.

HAZARD WARNING: *PHOSPHORUS(V) CHLORIDE REACTS VIOLENTLY WITH WATER.*
                        SOME OF ITS REACTIONS PRODUCE VERY IRRITATING
                        VAPOURS.
                        CONCENTRATED ACIDS ARE CORROSIVE.

RESIDUE DISPOSAL: *POUR RESIDUES INTO RUNNING WATER IN FUME CUPBOARD*
                        SINK.

In this exercise you will survey the range of reactions of carboxylic acids using simple test tube experiments.

ASSESSMENT: You are reminded of the general advice on what your teacher will be looking for in test tube observation and deduction work (see 1.2, 1.3 and 1.4). Ensure that you have carried out the instructions completely and carefully. Advice on techniques using organic reagents in test tube reactions is given in 2.2.5.

PROCEDURE: Carry out the tests described in Table 28 from the Teachers' Guide, recording your observations and deductions in the spaces provided in your copy of the table.

21.3 THE HYDROLYSIS OF AN ESTER.

HAZARD WARNING: *THE SODIUM HYDROXIDE IS HIGHLY CORROSIVE.*
    WEAR THE GLOVES PROVIDED.
    DON'T FORGET TO WEAR YOUR GOGGLES.

In this practical you will hydrolyse an aromatic ester and separate one of the products.

ASSESSMENT: You may be assessed on your manipulative skills (1.7). Refer to the use of apparatus with ground glass joints (2.4).

PROCEDURE:

(1)   Place 2.0 g of methyl 3-nitrobenzoate into a 50 cm^3 pear shaped flask.

(2)   Add 30 cm^3 of 6 mol dm^{-3} sodium hydroxide and fit the flask with a reflux condenser.

(3)   Reflux the mixture for half an hour over a gauze. Use a small flame.

(4)   Cool and carefully acidify the reaction mixture with dilute hydrochloric acid.

(5)   Filter the product, dry and weigh. Name this solid product.

(6)   Write an equation for the reaction using displayed formulae.

(7)   Calculate the percentage yield. Hand in your sample, clearly labelled with your melting point, percentage yield and your name.

21.4 ACID CHLORIDES AND ANHYDRIDES.

HAZARD WARNING: *ETHANOYL CHLORIDE IS VOLATILE AND FORMS PUNGENT*
    FUMES IN MOIST AIR. ETHANOIC ANHYDRIDE HAS A
    VERY PERSISTANT, IRRITATING VAPOUR.

In this exercise you will survey the range of reactions of acid chlorides and anhydrides using simple test tube experiments.

ASSESSMENT: You are reminded of the general advice on what your teacher will be looking for in test tube observation and deduction work (see 1.2, 1.3 and 1.4). Ensure that you have carried out the instructions completely and carefully. Advice on techniques using organic reagents in test tube reactions is given in 2.2.5.

PROCEDURE: Carry out the tests described in Table 29 from the Teachers' Guide, recording your observations and deductions in the spaces provided in your copy of the table. Write equations for the reactions involved in the deductions column.

21.5 PREPARATION OF PHENYL BENZOATE.

HAZARD WARNING: *BENZOYL CHLORIDE IS A LACHRYMATOR (Makes you cry!).*
    IT MUST BE HANDLED WITH CARE IN A FUME CUPBOARD.
    WEAR THE GLOVES PROVIDED, wash them well
    with soap and water before you take them off.
    REMEMBER PHENOL IS CORROSIVE, DO NOT ALLOW
    IT TO CONTACT YOUR SKIN.
    Wash away any spilt crystals immediately.

In this experiment you will prepare and purify a sample of a solid ester, phenyl benzoate. As phenol will not readily form an ester with a carboxylic acid, it is necessary to use an acid chloride. Hence benzoyl chloride is used instead of benzoic acid and an acid catalyst.

The phenol is first dissolved in sodium hydroxide and the solution is then treated with benzoyl chloride. The product is filtered and recrystallised from ethanol.

ASSESSMENT: You may be assessed on your manipulative skills (1.7). Refer to 2.5 for recrystallisation technique. Use of the Buchner funnel is in 2.6 and melting point determination in 2.7.

PROCEDURE:

(1) Place 2.5 g of phenol in a wide-mouthed 250 cm^3 reagent bottle and add 50 cm^3 of 2 mol dm^{-3} sodium hydroxide.

(2) Measure 4.5 cm^3 of benzoyl chloride into the reagent bottle, taking care not to spill any. Stopper the bottle firmly.

(3) Provided that there is no spilt benzoyl chloride on the outside of the bottle and it is tightly stoppered, it may be removed from the fume cupboard. Shake vigorously for fifteen minutes. If any lumps form, try to break these up by shaking. Alternatively use a glass rod.

(4) Now filter the white solid that has formed. Use a Buchner flask and funnel in the fume cupboard. Wash the solid well with water.

(5) Carefully transfer the crude solid to a 100 cm^3 conical flask and recrystallise it from the minimum quantity of hot ethanol.

(6) Cool well and collect the crystals, again using a Buchner flask and funnel. Dry thoroughly.

(7) Weigh the product and determine its melting point.

QUESTIONS:

(1) Write a balanced equation, using structural formulae for the reaction of phenol with sodium hydroxide.

(2) Write a balanced equation using structural formulae for the reaction of benzoyl chloride with the organic product from your first equation.

(3) What is the polarity of the carbonyl carbon in the benzoyl chloride? What kind of reagent will attack this carbon atom? Using your equations suggest a possible mechanism for the reaction.

(4) Calculate the percentage yield of phenyl benzoate. The density of benzoyl chloride is 1.21 g cm^{-3}. Hand in your sample clearly labelled with your name, percentage yield and melting point.

21.6 PREPARATION OF ASPIRIN.

HAZARD WARNING: *REMEMBER ETHANOIC ANHYDRIDE IS CORROSIVE AND HAS AN IRRITATING VAPOUR.*

The structure of aspirin is shown below, in the equation for its formation from 2-hydroxybenzoic acid.

This practical provides an opportunity to prepare a sample of aspirin using the same chemicals as the industrial process.

ASSESSMENT: You may be assessed on your manipulative skills (1.7). Refer to the use of apparatus with ground glass joints in 2.4. Recrystallisation technique is in 2.5, the use of the Buchner funnel in 2.6 and melting point determination in 2.7.

PROCEDURE:

(1) Place 2.0 g of 2-hydroxybenzoic (salicylic) acid in a 50 cm^3 pear shaped flask.

(2) Add 5 cm^3 of ethanoic anhydride and ten drops of concentrated phosphoric acid. Mix the contents carefully.

(3) Attach a reflux condenser to the flask and heat in a boiling water bath for about five minutes.

(4) Remove the water bath and pour 5 cm^3 of water down the condenser. The water will cause the excess of ethanoic anhydride to hydrolyse and the mixture will boil vigorously.

(5) When the hydrolysis has subsided, pour the contents of the flask into about 30 cm^3 of cold water in a beaker. Cool thoroughly and then filter the product using a Buchner flask and funnel. Wash sparingly with water.

(6) Recrystallise the product from the minimum quantity of boiling water.

(7) Filter and dry. Weigh your product and determine the percentage yield. Also determine the melting point. Place your sample in a tube labelled with your name, the percentage yield and melting point of your product. *YOUR PRODUCT IS NOT OF PHARMACEUTICAL QUALITY AND SHOULD ON NO ACCOUNT BE TAKEN.*

22. AMINES, AMIDES AND AMINO ACIDS

22.1 Introduction to organic nitrogen compounds.
22.2 Properties of amines and amides.
22.3 Properties of amino acids.

22.1 INTRODUCTION TO ORGANIC NITROGEN COMPOUNDS.

AIMS: This topic introduces you to the reactions of the amino group in amines, amides and amino acids.

THEORY: Like ammonia, the nitrogen of the amine group, $-NH_2$, has a lone pair of electrons. This lone pair enables dative covalent bonds to be formed to other groups. Thus amines act as bases, form complexes with transition metal ions and can react as nucleophiles.

All the amines studied here are primary amines, i.e. they have one of the hydrogen atoms in ammonia replaced by an organic group. Amines are very important compounds being used in the manufacture of drugs, dyes and nylon.

Amino acids are particularly interesting as a group of compounds. As well as their biological interest, they possess both an acidic group and a basic group within the same molecule. This gives rise to some properties which are not shown by either carboxylic acids or amines.

SUMMARY: At the end of this topic you should:

(1)   be familiar with the chemical reactions of amines and be able to explain these reactions and write balanced equations,

(2)   understand how the amine and carboxylic acid groups in an amino acid influence the properties of the amino acid.

LINKS: You will need a sound knowledge of the reactions of carboxylic acids (Topic 21) before studying amino acids. You should also know how to use acid and base dissociation constants (Topic 7).

22.2 PROPERTIES OF AMINES AND AMIDES.

HAZARD WARNING: *PHENYLAMINE IS TOXIC. IT IS ABSORBED THROUGH THE SKIN. AMINES ARE INFLAMMABLE AND, LIKE AMMONIA, GIVE OFF HARMFUL VAPOURS. PHENOL IS CORROSIVE AND TOXIC BY SKIN ABSORPTION.*

In this practical you will study the properties of the amine, $-NH_2$, and amide, $-CO-NH_2$, functional groups. The lone pair of electrons on the nitrogen atom in these compounds gives rise to reactions typical of bases. The different organic groups affect their relative strengths as bases.

ASSESSMENT: You may be assessed on your planning skills (1.6), your observations (1.3) or on your interpretation of the results (1.4) of this practical.

PROCEDURE: You are provided with samples of an aliphatic amine (ethylamine or butylamine), an aromatic amine (phenylamine), an amide (ethanamide) and a concentrated aqueous solution of ammonia. Read through the following instructions and prepare a suitable table for recording all that you do, observe and deduce.

(1)   Investigate the relative solubilities of these compounds in water and determine the order of their strength as bases. You are provided with full range indicator solution. Suggest, in outline only, what further experiments are needed to be certain that the order of base strength that you have observed is correct.

128

(2) Treat small samples of the compounds with dilute hydrochloric acid. Record what you observe. Evaporate the resulting solutions and describe the residues. What can you deduce from your observations? How could you recover an amine or an amide from one of these residues? Try your suggestion with the phenylamine residue and describe what you observe.

(3) Add each of the compounds in turn to aqueous copper(II) sulphate and describe what you observe. Use your knowledge of the reaction of ammonia with copper sulphate to suggest explanations of your observations with the organic compounds.

(4) REACTIONS OF AMINES WITH NITROUS ACID. Carry out the tests described in Table 30 from the Teachers' Guide, recording your observations and deductions in the spaces provided.

22.3 PROPERTIES OF AMINO ACIDS.

In this practical glycine, $NH_2CH_2CO_2H$, is used to investigate the effect of the two functional groups on the properties of an amino acid.

ASSESSMENT: You may be assessed on your observations (1.3) or on your deductions (1.4).

PROCEDURE:

(1) In order to see clearly the effect of the glycine in these tests a control is necessary for each test. Use pure water for your control. Dissolve a spatula full of glycine in about 20 cm^3 of pure water for your amino acid solution and use a few cm^3 of this for each test. You will need to record your results in an appropriate format.

(2) Determine the pH of the aqueous glycine and of the control.

(3) Add dropwise 0.1 mol dm^{-3} hydrochloric acid to the aqueous glycine and to the control in the presence of Universal indicator solution. Continue the addition until there is no further change.

(4) Add dropwise 0.1 mol dm^{-3} sodium hydroxide to the aqueous glycine and to the control, again in the presence of Universal indicator solution. Continue the addition until there is no further change.

(5) Add about 1 cm^3 aqueous copper sulphate to the aqueous glycine and to the control.

(6) By comparing the observations that you have made with the glycine and the control, explain any differences in behaviour. You should consider how the reagent used will interact with the functional groups on the glycine. Write equations for any reactions involved.